D0732058

Classroom Management & Assessment

Titles in the Proven Programs in Education Series

Classroom Management and Assessment

Literacy (coming in 2015)

*Science, Technology,
and Mathematics (STEM)*

Social and Emotional Health (coming in 2015)

Proven Programs in Education

Classroom Management & Assessment

Robert E. Slavin
Editor

Foreword by Marcia L. Tate

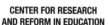

JOHNS HOPKINS
SCHOOL *of* EDUCATION
CENTER FOR RESEARCH
AND REFORM IN EDUCATION

UNIVERSITY *of York*

Institute for
Effective Education

CORWIN
A SAGE Company

CORWIN
A SAGE Company

FOR INFORMATION:

Corwin
A SAGE Company
2455 Teller Road
Thousand Oaks, California 91320
(800) 233-9936
www.corwin.com

SAGE Publications Ltd.
1 Oliver's Yard
55 City Road
London, EC1Y 1SP
United Kingdom

SAGE Publications India Pvt. Ltd.
B 1/I 1 Mohan Cooperative Industrial Area
Mathura Road, New Delhi 110 044
India

SAGE Publications Asia-Pacific Pte. Ltd.
3 Church Street
#10–04 Samsung Hub
Singapore 049483

Executive Editor: Arnis Burvikovs
Associate Editor: Desirée A. Bartlett
Editorial Assistant: Ariel Price
Production Editor: Melanie Birdsall
Copy Editor: Megan Markanich
Typesetter: Hurix Systems Pvt. Ltd.
Proofreader: Caryne Brown
Indexer: Judy Hunt
Cover Designer: Anupama Krishnan
Marketing Manager: Lisa Lysne

Copyright © 2014 by Corwin

All rights reserved. When forms and sample documents are included, their use is authorized only by educators, local school sites, and/or noncommercial or nonprofit entities that have purchased the book. Except for that usage, no part of this book may be reproduced or utilized in any form or by any means, electronic or mechanical, including photocopying, recording, or by any information storage and retrieval system, without permission in writing from the publisher.

All trade names and trademarks recited, referenced, or reflected herein are the property of their respective owners who retain all rights thereto.

Printed in the United States of America

Library of Congress Cataloging-in-Publication Data

Classroom management and assessment / Robert E. Slavin, Editor.

pages cm.—(Proven programs in education)

"Proven Programs in Education is a series of books that draws on the best of Better: Evidence-Based Education"—Publisher.

Includes bibliographical references and index.

ISBN 978-1-4833-5120-9 (pbk.)

1. Classroom management—Case studies. 2. Educational tests and measurements—Case studies. I. Slavin, Robert E. II. Better.

LB3013.C5273 2014

371.102'4—dc23

2013051357

This book is printed on acid-free paper.

SUSTAINABLE FORESTRY INITIATIVE
Certified Chain of Custody
Promoting Sustainable Forestry
www.sfiprogram.org
SFI-01268

SFI label applies to text stock

14 15 16 17 18 10 9 8 7 6 5 4 3 2 1

Contents

Foreword   vii
  Marcia L. Tate

Introduction   ix

Preface   x
  Robert Slavin

About the Editor   xii

Chapter 1. Assessment in a Differentiated Classroom   1
  Carol Ann Tomlinson and Tonya Moon

Chapter 2. Formative Assessments in High Schools   6
  Douglas Fisher and Nancy Frey

Chapter 3. Formative Assessment and Feedback to Learners   11
  Steve Higgins

Chapter 4. Multiple Measures in Classroom Assessment   16
  Susan Brookhart

Chapter 5. Promoting Learning and Achievement Through Self-Assessment   20
  Heidi Andrade

Chapter 6. Exposing the Imbalance in "Balanced Assessment"   25
  W. James Popham

Chapter 7. Do We Need an Assessment Overhaul?   30
  Jay McTighe and Grant Wiggins

Chapter 8. Formative Assessment: An Enabler of Learning   35
  Margaret Heritage

Chapter 9. Upgrading High-Stakes Assessments   39
  Albert Oosterhof

Chapter 10. England Versus Wales: Education Performance and Accountability   45
  Sandra McNally

Chapter 11. In Search of Feasible Fidelity   50
  David Andrews

Chapter 12. Before Choosing, Ask Three Questions   55
Steve Fleischman

Chapter 13. What Works in Classroom Management   60
Thomas Kratochwill, Rachel DeRoos, and Samantha Blair

Chapter 14. Good Instruction Is Good Classroom Management   66
Robert Slavin

Chapter 15. Am I the Only One Struggling With Classroom Management?   71
Inge Poole and Carolyn Evertson

Chapter 16. Classroom Management: What Teachers Should Know   76
Regina Oliver

Chapter 17. From Tourists to Citizens   80
H. Jerome Freiberg

Chapter 18. Promoting Engagement With Check & Connect   85
Angie Pohl and Karen Storm

Chapter 19. Dealing With Classroom Management Problems   90
Saul Axelrod

Chapter 20. Support for Teachers Around the World   94
Judy Hutchings

Chapter 21. Positive Behavioral Interventions and Supports   99
Catherine Bradshaw

Chapter 22. First Step to Success for Preschool Children   105
Edward Feil, Andy Frey, and Annemieke Golly

Chapter 23. Improving Teaching in Science and Mathematics   110
Claudia Fischer and Karen Rieck

Chapter 24. Improving Reading and Math Achievement Across a Whole District   116
Allen Thurston, Peter Tymms, Christine Merrell, and Nora Conlin

Chapter 25. Co-Teaching: Inclusion and Increased Student Achievement   121
Marilyn Friend and Tammy Barron

**Chapter 26. Implementing Response to Instruction
and Intervention With Older Students**   126
Nancy Frey and Douglas Fisher

Chapter 27. Teaching English Language Learners in Inclusion Settings   131
Kristi Santi and David Francis

Index   137

Foreword

It is only fitting that the articles contained in this anthology are updated from a previous publication called *Better* since you will not find a better treatment of two timely topics in education: classroom management and assessment. Credentialed academicians from around the world share their research-based findings in a plethora of twenty-seven brief but informative articles.

If teachers wait until they have planned their lessons to determine how they will assess their students, then they have waited too long. The assessment articles in this book go a long way toward answering the question *How do we know they are learning?* The first part shares best practices for making assessment results count. The articles begin with the importance of both pre-assessment and formative assessment to determine what students should *know, understand,* and be able to *do* (KUD). Other chapters delineate specific ways that teachers can check for understanding and the importance of feedback in the entire process as well as the need for multiple measures of assessment, including self-assessment. One article questions the merit of interim assessments since their use does not appear to be research based. Another questions something I have always wondered—whether the overemphasis on standardized testing is actually at odds with the reason students should be coming to school in the first place: more meaningful learning.

Classroom management is not everything, but it makes everything else possible! This statement is validated in the second half of this book. One very practical article espouses that the best defense against classroom management problems is an engaging lesson. Another gives specific ways to structure an effective learning environment so that many behavior problems are avoided. Such research-based programs as Classroom Organization and Management Program (COMP) at Vanderbilt University, Consistency Management & Cooperative Discipline (CMCD) from the University of Houston, Check & Connect from the University of Minnesota, and applied behavioral analysis (ABA) from Temple University are delineated. Another chapter relates the need for both pre-service and in-service teacher preparation programs if teachers are to become competent while yet another finds the solution to classroom management concerns in Positive Behavioral Interventions and Supports (PBIS).

In my more than forty years in education, where more than twenty-five of those years involved teaching teachers and administrators, I have come to one conclusion. Educators need and want two things. First, they need to know what research-based practices truly work for students. The articles in this book contain a plethora of this type of information. Second, educators want to definitively know how to practically apply the research in a school or classroom come Monday morning. Other articles in the book address just that. When some of the most renowned and respected research-based educators in the world share their best thinking in one resource, that resource should definitely become a part of every educator's professional library. I will certainly add it to mine!

—*Marcia L. Tate*
Educational Consultant
Developing Minds, Inc.

Introduction

In 2009 a new journal was launched by the Center for Research and Reform in Education at the Johns Hopkins School of Education and the Institute for Effective Education at the University of York in the United Kingdom. Called *Better: Evidence-Based Education,* this unique publication aims to get the latest education research into the hands of the people who need it, particularly teachers, administrators, and policy makers.

Each issue of the journal features accessible articles written by leading international academics, all of which are rooted in what really works in the classroom. The articles that have been published in *Better* form an invaluable anthology of the latest developments in evidence-based education, and so we decided to bring them together in a series of themed books. This book comprises articles on the subject of classroom management and assessment, all reviewed by the original authors and, where necessary, updated. We hope you find it useful.

Preface

How can teachers create classroom environments in which students are productively engaged at all times? Classrooms in which time is effectively used? In which activities are structured to maximize motivation and deep learning? In which behavioral disruptions are mostly prevented and responded to effectively if they do occur?

How can teachers assess student learning—both formatively during instruction and summatively at the end of a lesson or unit? How can they use innovative approaches to assessment to encourage learning behaviors that go beyond lower-level skills and facts? How can assessment be embedded in tasks so that teachers and students constantly learn how students are progressing toward class objectives and standards?

These and many other questions about classroom management and assessment are at the core of effective teaching. These are two of the issues that teachers worry most about, and there are dozens of books on each. What is distinctive about this one?

The answer is that in this volume, respected researchers have written about *what works* in classroom management and assessment. That is, they are not writing uninformed ideas about how classrooms could be managed and learning assessed but are writing about strategies that have been put to the test in real classrooms and found to improve learning and behavior.

In education today, evidence of effectiveness is becoming increasingly important. Educational leaders don't just want to know what's "in"; they want to know what works. Ideally, what this means is that innovative practices or programs have been tested in experiments, in which some number of teachers use the new practices while others continue with their usual practices. All students are tested before and after the experiment. If the classes using the new methods show greater gains, this is good evidence that the practice is effective. If many such studies find similar impacts, the body of evidence grows, and educators can have increasing confidence that the practice is likely to be beneficial in their classrooms, too.

The classroom management and assessment methods described in this book have been proven to work, sometimes in dozens of studies collectively involving hundreds of teachers. Because different researchers use different methods, and because science progresses over time, not all of the chapters agree with each other. However, basic principles of effective practice in classroom management and assessment have been supported many times and appear across many individual chapters.

The chapters in this book are updates of articles that first appeared in a journal called *Better: Evidence-Based Education. Better* is produced three times a year in a collaboration between the Institute for Effective Education at the University of York, in England, and the Center for Research and Reform in Education at the Johns Hopkins School of Education. Each issue is on a particular topic, and top researchers on that topic are invited to submit articles intended to translate their own research or reviews of their field into language that is accessible to practicing educators and educational leaders. Authors were asked to include compelling classroom examples to make their findings clear and pragmatic. We did not want authors to hold back on the richness of their ideas but just to express them in a nonacademic way.

As editor-in-chief of *Better,* I have the job of inviting researchers to submit articles. These are very busy, productive, and sought-after people, yet they hardly ever refuse. In fact, I think most authors are delighted to have a place to explain to educators the meaning of what they have spent their professional lives trying to learn about. These are people who care deeply about teaching, teachers, and learning, not just about theory. I think that's why they have been delighted to set aside their usual academic work for a while to write for the professionals on the front lines.

This book is the product of the talents of many people. I'd like to thank all of the researchers who have contributed to *Better:* to Jonathan Haslam, Jeannette Bollen-McCarthy, and Bette Chambers at the University of York; to Beth Comstock at Johns Hopkins University; and to Arnis Burvikovs at Corwin.

Funding for *Better* and for the creation of this book was provided by the Bowland Charitable Trust, whose trustee, Tony Cann, is never satisfied until research makes a difference in the lives of children. This is a value shared by everyone involved in this enterprise.

—*Robert Slavin*

About the Editor

 **Robert E. Slavin** is the director of the Center for Research and Reform in Education at the Johns Hopkins School of Education; a professor in the Institute for Effective Education at the University of York; and the driving force behind the Success for All Foundation, a nonprofit organization dedicated to the development, evaluation, and dissemination of research-proven reform models for preschool, elementary, middle, and high schools—especially those serving many children considered at risk.

Assessment in a Differentiated Classroom

Carol Ann Tomlinson and Tonya Moon

Assessment at every stage of instruction can help teachers match teaching and learning plans to students' learning needs. **Carol Ann Tomlinson** *and* **Tonya Moon** *explain.*

Architects are advisers in the building process, making a complex system manageable by formulating critical decisions, setting quantifiable results, and working closely with others while encouraging colleagues to employ the industry's best practices. The role of the teacher is not dissimilar. The teacher, too, works in a complex system serving as a change agent for students. An effective teacher makes the curriculum (the "what" of teaching) accessible through appropriate instructional practices (the "how" of teaching).

The teacher's role is made more complex by the reality of student diversity in readiness to learn, language, economic background, culture, motivation, interests, approach to learning, and so on. How well the teacher serves as a change agent for the full range of students in the complex system we call a classroom is both measured and informed by persistent use of assessment. In a differentiated classroom, generation and use of data to inform instruction, as well as to measure the effectiveness of instruction, is a core part of the instructional cycle and is critical to the success of both teacher and students.

The collection and use of assessment data to support differentiation occurs in three stages:

- Planning for instruction, including pre-assessment
- Implementing instruction, including formative assessment
- Evaluating instruction, including summative assessment

Stage I: Planning for Instruction, Including Pre-Assessment

Know, Understand, and Be Able to Do

Fundamental to the success of the teaching and learning process is a teacher's clarity about what students must know, understand, and be able to do (KUD) as the result of each segment of learning. KUDs provide teacher and students with clarity about learning targets and also facilitate alignment of teaching, learning, assessment, and differentiation. KUDs should provide a framework that engages learners and promotes their understanding of key content. Engagement is essential for sustained student motivation. Understanding is critical for student retention, application, and transfer of what they learn. KUDs also provide parameters for differentiation because the goal is rarely different content for different learners but rather different approaches to, and support systems for, mastering required content.

Pre-Assessments

With KUDs clearly established, teachers can create pre-assessments that measure a student's current status with target KUDs and critical prerequisites that teachers might otherwise assume students bring to class from past school experiences. Pre-assessment can also expose students' misconceptions about content, cueing teachers to address those barriers. In addition, pre-assessments can be valuable in revealing students' interests, enabling teachers to make content more relevant and helping teachers grow their understanding of the range of ways in which their students might approach learning most efficiently.

Pre-assessments can take many forms, including journal entries, Frayer Models, concept maps, short answer "tests," and interest surveys, to name a few. Students should understand that pre-assessments are not graded but serve the purpose of helping the teacher plan how best to move them forward in the unit of study. Teachers in effectively differentiated classrooms use pre-assessment data to select materials to appropriately challenge their students; assign students to groups based on readiness, interest, and learning preferences; plan for small-group instruction; and so on. Pre-assessments help teachers understand the variety of needs in their classrooms as the study of content begins in order to quickly optimize the match between learner need and teacher instruction.

Stage 2: Implementing Instruction and Formative Assessment

Teacher Role

Once initial instructional plans are informed through the use of pre-assessment information and a unit of study unfolds, the second phase of data-informed instructional planning begins. The teacher in a differentiated classroom regularly uses both formal and informal formative assessment to chart the progress of each learner—and of the class as a whole—toward achieving the designated goals. As with pre-assessment, alignment of formative or ongoing assessment—and the instruction that follows with KUDs—is essential. While formative assessment should rarely be used for grading purposes, it is important for teachers to provide students with specific feedback from ongoing assessment in order both to help them understand their own progress and to more readily and accurately contribute to their own academic growth.

Ongoing assessments can be informal (e.g., making observations of or having discussions with students as they work, taking notes during small-group instruction, asking students to indicate their comfort level with a skill through use of hand signals) or formal (e.g., Frayer Models, exit cards, entry cards, writing prompts, systematic use of checklists to monitor student development of knowledge or skill). Data from formative assessments provide a compass for the teacher for forward-planning, in terms of how various students might best access ideas and information, what types of class and homework tasks will serve particular students most effectively at a given time, how to use flexible grouping most effectively, which students need additional support, how to pace instruction, and so on.

Student Role

Best practice suggests that the role of students in formative assessment should extend beyond being the subject of observation. Not only is it important that students be clear about criteria that will indicate success on assessments but also that teachers involve them in developing those criteria so that they are more attuned to and invested in their own success. Likewise, having students evaluate their own formative work according to specified KUDs and carefully developed rubrics can further support learning efficacy. When students get feedback that supports and guides, rather than judges, they are more likely to develop realistic perceptions about their status and to develop the belief that persistent effort on their part contributes to their success as learners. In other words, formative assessment can and should contribute to what Carol Dweck (2006) calls a "growth mind-set"—the belief that people can make themselves smarter and more successful through sustained effort.

Stage 3: Evaluating Instruction and Summative Assessment

There are times when teachers seek evidence of understanding in a summative way. Summative assessments are graded and appropriately occur at transitional points, such as the end of a unit, the end of a marking period, or the end of a semester. Once again, summative assessment should be tightly aligned to the specified KUDs that have guided curriculum design, pre-assessment, instructional decisions, and formative assessment. Summative assessment data help students benchmark their growth and allow teachers to determine mastery of content. While summative assessment has a "final" aspect, it, too, is somewhat formative in nature. Teachers can look for patterns in achievement that suggest the need for modification the next time they teach the content. Students can look ahead from summative assessment to the next opportunities to apply skills or understandings they have—or have not—mastered.

Differentiation

Differentiation can play a role in summative assessments, whether they are closed or performance based. The purpose of an assessment is to reveal what a student knows, understands, and can do related to a set of clearly defined objectives (KUDs). If an English language learner (ELL) understands the process of photosynthesis but is unable to demonstrate that mastery in a test because it requires an essay response, the test has failed to reveal what the student knows. It would have been helpful to offer the option of writing an essay, completing a structured chart, or presenting a series of annotated storyboards.

Summative assessments can be differentiated in terms of complexity of the language of directions, providing varied options for expressing learning, degree of structure versus independence required for the task, the nature of resource materials, and so on. What cannot be differentiated is the set of criteria that determine success. In other words, with the exception of students whose educational plans indicate otherwise, the KUDs established at the outset of a unit remain constant for all students.

Conclusion

The teacher in a differentiated classroom is an architect of instruction designed to maximize the success of all learners. Assessment allows the teacher to be a successful change agent, working on behalf of students to understand their development as learners and to use best practices to scaffold their growth from varied points of readiness, interest, and approach to learning.

What We Know

- Pre-assessment and formative assessment are critical tools in designing instruction that addresses varied learner needs.
- Student achievement benefits when teachers use pre-assessment and formative assessment data to plan instruction to address learner needs.
- Student investment in learning and achievement benefit when students know the learning goals and use feedback from formative assessment to achieve those goals.

About the Authors

Carol Ann Tomlinson is the William Clay Parrish Jr. Professor and chair of Educational Leadership, Foundations, and Policy at the University of Virginia's Curry School of Education. She was also a public school educator for 20 years. Her work focuses on differentiated instruction.

Tonya Moon is a professor at the University of Virginia's Curry School of Education. Her interests and work focus on student assessment and the development of talent in school-age children.

References and Further Reading

Black, P., & Wiliam, D. (1998). Inside the black box: Raising standards through classroom assessment. *Phi Delta Kappan, 80,* 139–148.

Dweck, C. (2006). *Mindset: The new psychology of success.* New York: Ballantine.

Earl, L. (2003). *Assessment as learning: Using classroom assessment to maximize student learning.* Thousand Oaks, CA: Corwin.

Stiggins, R. J., Arter, J. A., Chappuis, J., & Chappuis, S. (2004). *Classroom assessment for student learning: Doing it right—using it well.* Portland, OR: Assessment Training Institute.

Tomlinson C. A., & Moon T. R. (2013). *Assessment and student success in a differentiated classroom.* Alexandria, VA: ASCD.

Formative Assessments in High Schools

Douglas Fisher and Nancy Frey

Douglas Fisher and **Nancy Frey** *describe a four-step approach to successful formative assessment.*

Teachers who use formative assessment target their instruction to student needs. Teachers who do not use formative assessments rely on guesswork or generic plans, rather than basing their instructional decisions on data. The difference in student learning is striking. Simply said, the systematic use of formative assessments results in better learning.

As a quick comparison, formative and summative assessments differ in terms of when they are administered, how often they are used, and what is done with the results (see Figure 2.1). While both are useful in teaching and learning, our focus here is on formative assessments that are useful in planning instructional interventions.

Formative assessments work when they are systematic and purposeful. The unfocused use of random data collection tools cannot yield focused instruction. Teachers have a lot of data about students, some of which are useful in planning and some of which are not. What teachers need is a system for effectively using student performance data to make instructional decisions, rather than another test. We have developed such a system with four components: feeding up, checking for understanding, giving feedback, and feeding forward.

Feeding Up

As part of any formative assessment system, both teacher and students have to understand the purpose of the lesson and the purpose of the assessment. A clear purpose should be communicated with students on a daily basis. In addition to

Figure 2.1   Differences Between Formative and Summative Assessments

Differences	Formative Assessments	Summative Assessments
When administered	Daily, if not more often	At the conclusion of a unit of study
Frequency of use	Ongoing, regularly	Typically once or twice per unit of study
Use of results	Inform teacher about effectiveness of lessons; plan teaching; identify students in need of immediate additional support	Grades; accountability systems; inform teacher about effectiveness of teaching or intervention; identify students in need of long-term support

staying focused on the topic, a clear purpose allows the teacher to determine when learning targets have been met. For example, consider the following two purpose statements:

- To understand the causes and effects of World War II
- To explain why the attack on Pearl Harbor resulted in the United States' entry into World War II

The first statement is too broad, as it will take many lessons to meet this objective. The second highlights what students should learn on a specific day and provides the teacher with information about what to assess. With a clear purpose, communicated with students, teachers are ready for the second component.

Checking for Understanding

There are a number of excellent ways that teachers can check for student understanding, including the following:

- *Oral language,* such as inviting students to explain how they solved an algebra problem, putting their thumbs up or down to indicate agreement with a prediction during a science experiment, or holding up a yes or no response card when asked about a character's actions in a play.
- *Questions,* including those that require critical thinking, such as "compare and contrast the roles of Snowball and Napoleon in *Animal Farm.*" Questions can be oral or written and may include a range of student responses from recall to synthesis.
- *Writing,* such as "exit slips" in which students summarize their understanding of sources or respond to prompts such as the following: "How are we connected to our environment?"
- *Projects and performances,* through which students demonstrate their understanding, such as an erosion map in earth science or an enactment of a play.

- *Quizzes and tests,* which are used to plan instruction rather than provide students with a grade. In the case of formative assessments, each of the distracter items should be diagnostic in terms of student understanding. For example, one of the wrong choices for an algebra problem might be based on choosing the wrong algorithm, whereas another choice might be based on common mathematical errors, such as forgetting to change the number from negative to positive when squaring.

Giving Feedback

When the teacher has formative assessment data, students expect feedback. For feedback to be effective, it must be timely, specific, and understandable. However, even when those conditions are met, feedback by itself has limited impact on student understanding and thus achievement. If you doubt this, check the trash can (or recycling bin) following a lesson, and you will find examples of student work on which the teacher has written a great deal of useful information. The teacher has worked hard, providing students with information about their performance, but it has gone to waste.

In a formative assessment system, students receive feedback that is more global in nature. The specifics are left for feed-forward, which we will focus on next. For example, on an essay, a student received the following comment from his teacher: "Your transitions and organization have significantly improved. The next area of attention might be word choice. You express your ideas well and could make a stronger case with increased academic vocabulary." In addition, the student received a rubric with specific areas identified and a grade on the paper. This feedback focused on what the student had demonstrated successfully, based on previous instruction, and what the student might focus on next. In addition, the rubric provided feedback about specific aspects of the paper, such as mechanics, thesis development, and so on. Of course there was also a summative component and a grade.

Feeding Forward

Unfortunately, too many teachers use feedback as their entire formative assessment system. This transfers all of the responsibility for learning to the student and fails to provide the teacher with specific teaching points. Remember that the power of a formative assessment system is that it can inform the teacher about next steps for instruction. The feed-forward element of this formative assessment system ensures that data are collected and analyzed for patterns so that the teacher can make informed decisions about what should be taught next.

An error analysis sheet is a vital tool for feeding forward. When teachers provide students with targeted feedback, as in the previous example, they have time to focus on the errors students make. But the next step is to record this feedback for analysis—for example, the error analysis sheet a social studies teacher created as she was teaching her students to read primary source documents (see Figure 2.2). The teacher

Figure 2.2 Error Analysis in History

Date: 10/12
Topic: Reading primary sources

Error	Period 1	Period 2	Period 3	Period 4	Period 5
Skimming and scanning; previewing text	JC			AA	
Predicting errors	JC, JT, AG, DL, TV	EC, MV, WK		AA, SK, MG, EM, BA, TS	HH, DP, MR, CH
Making connections	JC, AG, SL	WK, MW		AA, BA	MR
Sourcing	JC, JT, DL, MM, SL, ST, ND	RT, VE, VD, CC		AA, MG, SC, PM, LG	DP, DE
Drawing conclusions	JC, JT, MM	EC, SJ		AA, MG, BA, GL, PT, DO, DE, LR, SK, EM, TS, LG, PM, DP, RT, HA, KJ, DE, RC, DW, DL, KS, IP, SN, MW, JG, KE, JV	DE, MR, DC, AT

identified errors her students were making, listed them on a code sheet, and entered students' initials in the corresponding place on the table. In this way, she was able to focus on trend data, which gave her an actionable plan. It is clear that the fourth period needs a great deal more instruction on drawing conclusions. This is considered a global error, given that more than 60 percent of the students in the class made this same error. The other identified errors are targeted errors, and the students who made them need additional small-group support. The trend data also identify students, such as JC in first period and AA in fourth period, who need intensive interventions if they are to be successful in this class. This analysis of student work has led teachers to specific actions they can take to plan instruction and meet student needs.

Conclusion

The error analysis sheet is a concrete example of the ways in which a formative assessment system can be used to plan instruction. Having said that, it is important to note that this was not done in isolation. The students and their teacher understood the purpose of the lesson and the assessment, and the teacher checked for understanding throughout the lesson and collected data to analyze. Had she simply identified errors, nothing much would have changed in terms of student understanding. The feed-forward aspect of the formative assessment system provided the teacher with information about which students needed to be taught next. Taken together, the formative assessment links student work with instruction such that better learning occurs.

What We Know

- Formative assessment systems are based on student performance and provide teachers with data about what to teach next.
- Feedback is not effective in isolation; rather, it needs to be acted on by both students and teachers.
- Checking for understanding, based on a clear purpose, is an important part of a formative assessment system and should not be overlooked.

About the Authors

Douglas Fisher and **Nancy Frey** are professors of educational leadership at San Diego State University and teacher leaders at Health Sciences High and Middle College in San Diego, California. They focus their research on quality teaching, including the use of assessment information to inform instruction.

References and Further Reading

Fisher, D., & Frey, N. (2007). *Checking for understanding: Formative assessments for your classroom.* Alexandria, VA: ASCD.

Frey, N., & Fisher, D. (2011). *The formative assessment action plan: Practical steps to more successful teaching and learning.* Alexandria, VA: ASCD.

Hattie, J., & Timperley, H. (2007). The power of feedback. *Review of Educational Research, 77,* 81–112.

Formative Assessment and Feedback to Learners

Steve Higgins

Feedback to students is at the heart of successful teaching, but research suggests that how *this is given is key to whether it is effective.* **Steve Higgins** *explains.*

I work closely with teachers and am passionate about supporting them with research evidence that is helpful and practical for their teaching. Recently I have been undertaking a review of the evidence about what works for learners for the Sutton Trust, a U.K. charity that aims to improve educational opportunities for children and adolescents from nonprivileged backgrounds and to increase social mobility. One of the questions that teachers have frequently asked me is about what works in terms of formative assessment and feedback to students.

Assessment and Learning

Feedback is an essential part of the learning process, but both students and teachers are often disappointed or even frustrated at the feedback process. Students complain they don't know what to do when they get the results of assessments or even say getting feedback is demoralizing. More critically, they often say that feedback comes too late to be of any use to them at all.

One of the aims of assessment and testing of students in the classroom is that it should help teachers teach more effectively, by making them understand what their students already know or can do. It should also help students understand what they have to do next to improve their own learning. Thought of in this way, feedback is not one-sided; it is a transaction between teacher and learner.

Formative Assessment and "Assessment for Learning"

In recent years there has been increasing interest in formative assessment where information is used by the teacher or by the learner as information to change what they do next in a teaching or learning activity. Assessment for learning is an assessment task in which the main purpose is to promote or improve students' learning. This is different from assessments that aim to hold schools or teachers accountable or to identify the competence or ranking of students. An assessment activity can help learning in this way only if it provides information that teachers and their students can use as feedback in assessing themselves and one another and then in modifying the teaching and learning activity. Assessment for learning becomes "formative assessment" only when it leads to this change.

We know that frequent summative tests and assessments have a negative impact on students' views of themselves as learners. This is especially true with "high-stakes" testing, when teachers may narrow the curriculum that they teach to match the test. This suggests that such assessments are more important for school or teacher accountability than for learning.

We know, too, that simply practicing assessments will improve students' performance, at least in the short term, but this does not help them with their learning. It's rather like squeezing a child's balloon; the bulge you make when you squeeze it makes the balloon look as if it is getting bigger, but there is really no more air in there. Once you let go, it goes back to the size it was before. Test practice is a bit like this in that the students aren't learning anything new. You are just squeezing the balloon. The way you get more air in the balloon is through more effective teaching. A key component of this is feedback that keeps teaching and learning on track to achieve its goals.

This suggests that a closer examination of feedback is needed. The analysis that follows focuses on what teachers can do in terms of *how* they give feedback to learners and *what* they get students to think about, rather than other parts of the feedback cycle (such as how they might alter their instruction, or how learners can give feedback to each other). It is based on a number of reviews but in particular John Hattie's analysis. His work indicates that there are different kinds of feedback to consider. These are about the task itself, about the process of the task or activity, about students' management of their own learning or their self-regulation, and about them as individuals and who they are. Research suggests that feedback is best directed at the first three levels. In addition, evidence shows the following:

- It should be about *challenging* tasks or goals (rather than easy ones).
- It is even more important for teachers to give *feedback about what is right* rather than what is wrong.
- Feedback should be as *specific* as possible and, ideally, compare what students are doing *right* now with what they have done *wrong* before.
- It should *encourage* students and not threaten their self-esteem.

Table 3.1 provides examples of levels and types of feedback.

Table 3.1 Levels and Types of Feedback

Feedback About	Examples	Key Points
The task	Feedback about how well the task is being achieved or performed, such as the following: • Indicating where correct responses are different from incorrect • Getting more or different information relevant to the task • Building more task knowledge • Prompts and direct cues	Feedback that focuses even more on correct than incorrect behaviors and that encourages the learner Being positive about errors as learning opportunities
The process	Feedback specific to the processes of learning, the how rather than the what, or relating and extending tasks such as identifying the following: • Connections between ideas • Strategies for spotting mistakes • Explicitly learning from mistakes • Cues to the learner about different strategies and errors	Identifying where in the process to focus attention to improve, relative to previous attempts
Self-regulation	How students monitor, manage, and regulate their actions toward the learning goal, such as the following: • Capability to identify feedback themselves and to self-assess • Willingness to put effort into seeking and dealing with feedback • Having confidence they are correct • Positive attributions about success *and* failure • How good they are at help-seeking	Needs to emphasize success at challenging activities through effort, focusing on specific strategies for self-regulation that led to their success Successfully corrected errors are a key part of this.

(Continued)

(Continued)

Feedback About	Examples	Key Points
The individual	Praise directed to the effort, self-regulation, engagement, or processes relating to task or performance: • For example: "You're really great because you have worked hard to complete this task by applying this concept" NOT "Good girl."	The most common but most dangerous kind of feedback tends to be too general and too personal. Feedback should rather emphasize what the individual has done (or could do), not who he or she is.

Source: Adapted from Hattie and Timperley (2007, pp. 87–97).

Conclusion

Successful feedback is that which leads to action on the part of the teacher or learner and closes the formative assessment loop. Teachers should be very specific about their feedback and what to do in response and should encourage students to see mistakes as opportunities to improve.

What We Know

- Feedback is central to the teaching and learning process and keeps it on track.
- It closes the loop between assessment for learning and formative assessment by enabling action by the teacher and/or learner.
- Letting students know when they get things right and why they are correct is even more important than pointing out mistakes or errors.
- Specific feedback is more useful than general, particularly where this relates to previous work students have done.
- Praise should be specific to what the student has done.
- Feedback should encourage and not demoralize learners.

About the Author

Steve Higgins is professor of education at Durham University in the United Kingdom. He has an interest in classroom interaction and the role of the teacher in supporting learning by developing metacognition and self-regulation, particularly where digital technologies are involved.

References and Further Reading

Black, P., Harrison, C., Lee, C., Marshall, B., & Wiliam, D. (2003). *Assessment for learning: Putting it into practice*. Buckingham, UK: Open University Press.

Black, P., Harrison, C., Lee, C., Marshall, B., & Wiliam, D. (2004). Working inside the black box: Assessment for learning in the classroom. *Phi Delta Kappan, 86*(1), 9–21.

Harlen, W., & Deakin-Crick, R. (2002). A systematic review of the impact of summative assessment and tests on students' motivation for learning. In *Research Evidence in Education Library*. London: EPPI-Centre, Social Science Research Unit, Institute of Education, University of London. Retrieved from http://eppi.ioe.ac.uk/cms/?tabid=108

Hattie, J. (2008). *Visible learning*. London: Routledge.

Hattie, J., & Timperley, H. (2007). The power of feedback. *Review of Educational Research, 77*(1), 81–112.

Higgins, S., Katsipataki, M., Kokotsaki, D., Coleman, R., Major, L. E., & Coe, R. (2013). *The Sutton Trust-Education Endowment Foundation teaching and learning toolkit*. London: Education Endowment Foundation. Retrieved from http://educationendowmentfoundation.org.uk/toolkit/

Kingston, N., & Nash, B. (2011). Formative assessment: A meta-analysis and call for research. *Educational Measurement: Issues and Practice, 30*(4), 28–37.

Kluger, A. N., & DeNisi, A. (1996). The effects of feedback interventions on performance: A historical review, a meta-analysis, and a preliminary feedback intervention theory. *Psychological Bulletin, 119*(2), 254–284.

Multiple Measures in Classroom Assessment

Susan Brookhart

Susan Brookhart explains the benefits of a "multiple measures" approach to assessment.

In education, the term *multiple measures* means basing a conclusion or a decision on more than one source of evidence. It should not be a surprise that multiple measures are important in education, because they certainly are in other areas. Have you ever been late for a doctor's appointment, rushed in, and found your blood pressure was high? Would you expect your doctor to prescribe medication for high blood pressure based on that one reading? Or have you ever sat on a committee? Would you expect the committee to decide on its strategy based on the opinion of only one member? Of course not.

But in education we often have to work hard to prevent people from making judgments based on one test score or other single piece of information. I hope this chapter will do two things: first, help you understand—and be able to explain to others—why multiple measures are important and second, help you learn to use multiple measures for both formative and summative classroom assessment.

Why Use Multiple Measures in Classroom Assessment?

The reason to use multiple measures in the classroom is to obtain better evidence about whatever you are trying to measure. Do you want to know about Ethan's understanding of colonial America? Or are you trying to work out Carmen's comprehension of the main themes in *To Kill a Mockingbird*? Perhaps you are interested in diagnosing where Jayden needs help in factoring quadratic equations? These classroom assessment occasions are all better met with multiple measures.

One way in which multiple measures help to obtain better information is that they boost reliability, reducing the chances that your assessment is uncharacteristic in some way (like high blood pressure after rushing to the doctor). Having more than one measure helps to even out little anomalies in performance that happen by chance. And reliability contributes to validity. There is obviously no way that evidence about achievement can be sound, can be valid, and can be the basis for well-founded decisions if it is unreliable.

Another way in which multiple measures help improve validity is by enriching the limited picture that any one sample of test questions or performance tasks gives. Carmen is reading *To Kill a Mockingbird,* and you need evidence of the sense she is making of this complex piece of literature. What are the themes? How did the author use plot, character, and setting together to create them? Does Carmen think any of these themes are important today? A set of test questions, a paper, and participation in a prepared debate together allows for a broader set of evidence about the wide variety of knowledge and skills involved in "understanding the themes in *To Kill a Mockingbird*" than any one of these measures alone.

Multiple Measures for Formative Assessment

Formative assessment is a systematic process through which teachers and students gather evidence of learning with the express goal of improving achievement. The measures used for this are typically informal classroom assessments. These help with both teacher feedback and student self-assessment and result in specific information to inform forward-planning.

An excellent way to incorporate multiple measures in formative assessment is to use a series of assessments, each based on one or more aspects of the ultimate learning goals. These would not be graded but generate feedback from teacher, peers, and/or self-evaluation. For certain kinds of tasks, this might be a series of similar assessments. For example, students learning to write descriptive paragraphs might write three of them, with the first two serving as practice. Based on the feedback they received each time, and on their own reflection, the final paragraph might result in a grade (summative assessment).

For other kinds of tasks, this might be a series of assessments giving students and teachers information on different aspects of the learning goals. Again, these would not be graded but would generate feedback from teacher, peers, and/or self-evaluation. For example, as part of their study of colonial America, students might write or answer questions about the founding of the English colonies, their various government structures and functions, trade and commerce, and so on. After receiving feedback (including self-reflection) on these various aspects of the unit, students should be equipped to study better for a unit test and do better on graded projects or performance assessments.

Multiple Measures for Summative Assessment

In the colonial America example, a final set of summative, graded assessments might include a test, project, and performance assessment. Unit goals for understanding and being able to explain the importance of historical figures, events, and developments in colonial America describe a multifaceted domain of learning. A unit test would be particularly suited to capturing knowledge of facts and concepts and the kind of thinking and application that brief essay questions can measure. A project—perhaps a term paper or presentation about an important historical figure—is a type of performance assessment and is particularly suited to capturing students' understanding of this person. This would be at the level of writing a research question, collecting and organizing information, and presenting it. Another performance assessment—perhaps a debate—might be used to measure students' ability to use historical information for reasoning, problem solving, and communicating. For example, students could take the points of view of opposing factions on a colonial issue.

If the teacher put together these three summative assessments to arrive at a final grade for students for the colonial America unit, they would have a richer picture of students' levels of achievement for the unit goals than if they used any one of these alone. For any one student, the three assessments yield more information about more aspects of what they were expected to learn than one assessment would yield. If the teacher averages the grades, using a mean or median, this is a *compensatory* use of multiple measures. That is, high performance on one assessment can compensate for low performance on another assessment.

Sometimes teachers differentiate assessment, allowing scores on one assessment to substitute for scores on another. This is a *complementary* use of multiple measures, and although it can be useful, it can easily be misapplied as well. Suppose the teacher in our colonial America example knew a certain student had a debilitating fear of speaking in public. For that student, she might well substitute (a complementary use of multiple measures) an essay arguing the point of view the student would have been assigned in the debate. This is a wise and fair accommodation, since speaking in public is not the learning goal.

However, suppose the teacher decided she would allow students to pick the best one of their three grades (test, project, debate) and use that for the whole unit grade. If the goal is a grade that accurately reflects the student's level of achievement for the unit, this complementary use of multiple measures is *not* wise or well founded. Information about different aspects of the learning goals is lost. In effect, the goal here becomes to use the highest grade, without regard to the information it conveys.

What We Know

- Used wisely, multiple measures in classroom assessment yield richer, more accurate evidence about student achievement than single measures alone.
- For formative assessment of a learning goal, use a series of practice assignments or assessments over various aspects of the learning domain. Make sure

students receive feedback (from teacher, peer, or self) that moves learning forward.

- For summative assessment of students' level of achievement of a learning goal, use several assessments that, taken together, better represent the expectations of the learning domain than one assessment could alone.

About the Author

Susan Brookhart, PhD, is an educational consultant. Her interests include formative and summative classroom assessment and the connection between classroom assessment and large-scale assessment. She is author or coauthor of sixteen books and over fifty articles on these topics.

References and Further Reading

Bernhardt, V. L. (1998, March). *Multiple measures. Invited monograph No. 4.* Oroville: California Association for Supervision and Curriculum Development. Retrieved from http://eff.csuchico.edu/downloads/MMeasure.pdf

Brookhart, S. M. (2009). The many meanings of "multiple measures." *Educational Leadership, 67*(3), 6–12.

Brookhart, S. M. (2011). *Grading and learning: Practices that support student achievement.* Bloomington, IN: Solution Tree.

Williamson, G. L. (2006). *Managing multiple measures.* Durham, NC: MetaMetrics.

Promoting Learning and Achievement Through Self-Assessment

Heidi Andrade

> *Self-assessment is a matter of students getting useful feedback from themselves, for themselves, says **Heidi Andrade.***

Research has shown that feedback can promote learning and achievement, yet most students typically get little constructive criticism on their works in progress. This scarcity of feedback is due, in large part, to the fact that few teachers have the luxury of regularly responding to each student's work. Fortunately, research also shows that students themselves can be useful sources of feedback by thinking about the quality of their own work rather than relying on their teacher as the sole source of evaluative judgments.

Student self-assessment is a process of *formative* assessment during which students reflect on the quality of their work, judge the degree to which it reflects explicitly stated goals or criteria, and revise accordingly. Please note the emphasis on the word *formative*. Self-assessment is done on work in progress in order to inform revision and improvement: it is not a matter of having students determine their own grades. Self-evaluation, in contrast, refers to asking students to grade their own work—perhaps as part of their final grade for an assignment. Given what we know about human nature, as well as findings from research regarding students' tendency to inflate self-evaluations when they will count toward grades, I subscribe to a purely formative type of student self-assessment.

The Purpose of Self-Assessment

The purpose of engaging students in careful self-assessment is to boost learning and achievement and to promote academic self-regulation, or the tendency to monitor and manage one's own learning. Research suggests that self-regulation and achievement are closely related: Students who set goals, make flexible plans to meet them, and monitor their own progress are also more likely to learn more and do better in school than students who do not. Self-assessment is a core element of self-regulation because it involves awareness of the goals of a task and checking one's progress toward them.

The Features of Self-Assessment

Although even young children are typically able to think about the quality of their own work, they do not always do so—perhaps because one or more necessary conditions are not present. In order for effective self-assessment to occur, students need to have the following:

- Awareness of the value of self-assessment
- Access to clear criteria on which to base the assessment
- A specific task or performance to assess
- Direct instruction in and assistance with self-assessment
- Practice
- Opportunities to revise and improve the task or performance

This list of conditions might seem prohibitive, but several of the key conditions previously listed, including direct instruction and practice, are commonly employed classroom practices. The second condition—access to clear criteria on which to base self-assessment—can be met by introducing a rubric or checklist.

There are a number of ways to engage students in effective self-assessment. In general, the process involves the following three steps:

1. *Articulate goals and expectations.* The goals and expectations for the task or performance are clearly articulated, either by the teacher, by the students, or both. Because students become better acquainted with the task at hand when they are involved in thinking about what counts, I often cocreate all or part of a rubric in class by analyzing examples of strong and weak pieces of student work.

2. *Self-assess.* Students make a first attempt at their assignment, be it an essay, word problem, lab report, fitness plan, speech, or self-portrait. They monitor their progress on the assignment by comparing their work to the criteria on the rubric or checklist. In my research on self-assessment of writing, I ask students to use colored pencils to underline key phrases in the rubric and then underline in their drafts the evidence of having met the standard articulated

by the phrase. For example, students underline "clearly states an opinion" in blue on their persuasive essay rubric, then underline their opinions in blue in their persuasive essay drafts. To assess one aspect of sentence fluency, they underline "sentences begin in different ways" in yellow on their rubric, use the same yellow pencil to circle the first word in every sentence in their essays, and then say the circled words out loud with an ear for repetition. If students find they have not met a particular standard, they write themselves a reminder to make improvements in their final drafts. This process is followed for each criterion on the rubric, with pencils of various colors. And it is quick: the whole process can take as little as one lesson or can be done as homework.

3. *Revise.* Students use the feedback from their self-assessments to guide revision. This last step is crucial. Students are savvy, and will not self-assess thoughtfully unless they know that their efforts can lead to opportunities to actually make improvements and possibly increase their grades.

The Value of Self-Assessment

Some research suggests that simply handing out and explaining a rubric may increase students' knowledge of the criteria for an assignment and help students produce work of higher quality—or it may not. Simply handing out a rubric does not guarantee much of anything. Actively involving students in using a rubric to self-assess their work, however, has been associated with noticeable improvements in students' performances in writing, social studies, mathematics, science, and external examinations. In each case, students were either engaged in written forms of self-assessment using journals, rubrics, checklists, or questionnaires, or oral forms of self-assessment, such as interviews and student-teacher conferences.

To date, the bulk of the research on self-assessment has been done on writing and mathematics. Studies of writing have revealed an association between rubric-referenced self-assessment and the quality of writing done by students in elementary and middle school. Of note is the fact that improvements in the conventions of language (grammar and spelling) tend to be negligible: the advances in students' writing were the result of stronger performance on substantive criteria such as ideas and content, organization, voice and tone, and plot development. Similarly, studies conducted in math classes found that students who were taught to self-assess outperformed other students on word problems. In both writing and math, the differences between the treatment and comparison groups were practically, as well as statistically, significant.

Conclusions and Encouragement

Student self-assessment can have powerful effects on achievement. The effect can be both short-term, as when self-assessment positively influences student performance on a particular assignment, as well as long-term, as students become more self-regulated in their learning. I encourage educators to take advantage of what we now know about self-assessment by doing the following:

- Articulate the criteria by which students assess their work.
- Teach students how to apply the criteria.
- Give feedback on the accuracy of their self-assessments, as needed.
- Give help in using the results of self-assessment to improve performance.
- Provide sufficient time for revision after self-assessment.
- Do not turn self-assessment into self-evaluation by counting it toward a grade.

Under these conditions, self-assessment can ensure that all students get the kind of feedback they need, when they need it in order to learn and achieve.

What We Know

- Self-assessment involves students in thinking about the quality of their own work, rather than relying on their teachers as the sole source of feedback.
- Studies have shown that teaching students to reflect on the quality of their work, judge the degree to which it reflects explicitly stated criteria, and revise are associated with meaningful improvements in their grades.

Author's Note

The article from which this chapter was taken is "Promoting Learning and Achievement Through Self-Assessment" (Andrade & Valtcheva, 2009).

About the Author

Heidi Andrade is an associate professor of educational psychology and the associate dean for academic affairs at the School of Education at the University at Albany. Her most recent book, coedited with Greg Cizek, is the *Handbook of Formative Assessment*.

References and Further Reading

Andrade, H. (2013). Classroom assessment in the context of learning theory and research. In J. H. McMillan (Ed.), *SAGE handbook of research on classroom assessment* (pp. 17–34). Thousand Oaks, CA: Sage.

Andrade, H., Du, Y., & Wang, X. (2008). Putting rubrics to the test: The effect of a model, criteria generation, and rubric-referenced self-assessment on elementary school students' writing. *Educational Measurement: Issues and Practices, 27*(2), 3–13.

Andrade, H., & Valtcheva, A. (2009). Promoting learning and achievement through self-assessment. *Theory Into Practice, 48*(1), 12–19.

Gregory, K., Cameron, C., & Davies, A. (2000). *Self-assessment and goal-setting.* Merville, British Columbia, Canada: Connection Publishing.

Exposing the Imbalance in "Balanced Assessment"

W. James Popham

*There are three elements to "balanced assessment," but **W. James Popham** argues that only two deserve their place.*

It is difficult to attend any sort of assessment-relevant educational conference these days without hearing someone extol the virtues of "balanced assessment." In the United States, what is typically being described by the proponents of balanced assessment is the application of three distinctive measurement strategies: *classroom assessments, interim assessments,* and *large-scale assessments.*

Balanced assessment, as is the case with "balanced" anything, sounds so delightfully defensible. Those who oppose balanced assessment are apt to be the sorts of villains who want "low standards" instead of "high standards" and who applaud "unreliable tests" instead of tests reeking of reliability. Whatever is balanced seems *a priori* to be wonderful, but in this case the term may be misleading.

The "Blessed Trinity" of Balanced Assessment

Briefly, the three measurement strategies of balanced assessment are as follows:

- *Classroom assessments,* typically teacher-made, are currently employed by most teachers for the purpose of grading their students or as motivators when urging students to "study hard for the upcoming test." Classroom assessments can also supply timely evidence whenever teachers use formative assessment.

- *Interim assessments* are usually purchased from commercial vendors but are sometimes created locally. These are standardized tests, typically administered by a district or a state, perhaps two or three times during the school year. Interim tests are intended to fulfill one of the following three measurement missions: (1) a predictive function, such as identifying students who are at risk of failing a subsequent high-stakes test; (2) an evaluative function, such as appraising the effectiveness of a recently concluded educational program; or (3) an instructional function, such as supplying teachers with instructionally useful diagnostic data regarding their students. Occasionally, interim tests are intended to supply evidence for more than one of these functions.
- *Large-scale assessments* are almost always created by assessment organizations, either for-profit or not-for-profit groups. In the United States, the most common examples of these sorts of tests are the annual accountability assessments administered by all U.S. states. Although large-scale assessments are used for purposes other than accountability, for instance, as college entrance exams, the large-scale tests associated with the balanced assessment are typically achievement tests intended for use in an accountability context.

A Party Crasher

Two of these types of assessment are supported by strong evidence, but one is trying to crash the measurement party without the proper admission credentials.

Classroom Assessments

It's not classroom assessments. Classroom assessments are supported by a formidable array of empirical evidence showing that, when used properly, they trigger substantial growth by students. When classroom assessments are used as part of formative assessment—a process wherein assessment-elicited evidence is used by teachers and/or students to make necessary adjustments in what they are doing—there is an abundance of empirical evidence to show that the formative assessment process is remarkably effective. In their seminal 1998 review of classroom assessment studies, Paul Black and Dylan Wiliam concluded that formative assessment works conclusively, it produces powerful gains in students' achievement, and it is sufficiently robust so that teachers can use it in a variety of ways yet still get glittering results. Subsequent empirical investigations continue to support the instructional payoffs of appropriately employed classroom assessments.

Large-Scale Assessments

Nor are large-scale assessments the party crashers. Large-scale tests, particularly those employed for accountability purposes, enjoy enormous support among both educational policy makers and the public at large. The public is increasingly demanding hard evidence that their schools are being successful and that their taxes are being well spent. Not placated by educators' reassurances, educational policy makers at all levels, local to national, are demanding hard, test-based evidence regarding students' achievement. Large-scale accountability tests supply such evidence and will remain in place until an incredulous citizenry becomes convinced that our schools are working.

Interim Assessments

However, in contrast to the other two types of assessment, interim assessments are neither supported by research evidence nor regarded by the public or policy makers as being of particular merit. Indeed, most members of the public and most policy makers don't even know that interim assessments exist.

The chief advocacy for including interim assessments as one of the three strategies of balanced assessment, not surprisingly, comes from the vendors who sell them. Many district-level administrators are desperate to prevent their schools from getting low scores on annual state accountability tests and so are swayed by the glowing words about the positive instructional payoffs that accompany commercially peddled interim tests. It is not surprising that many district officials purchase interim assessments for their teachers.

Yet at the 2010 annual meeting of the National Council on Measurement in Education in Denver, Judith Arter—based on her careful review of research studies regarding interim tests—concluded that no meaningful empirical support currently exists for interim assessments. Regretfully, she noted that "the amount of attention being put on having interim assessments in place saps resources from other formative practices supported by a much larger research base."

Accordingly, when it comes to the support associated with these three assessment approaches, one of them is blatantly out of balance with its assessment cousins.

A Serious Shortcoming?

Interim tests, other than being seen by some armchair analysts as "rounding out" the balanced assessment picture, come to us without compelling support, either empirical or political. In the United States, where almost any TV-advertised health product is accompanied these days by an allusion to "clinical evidence" supporting the product's virtues, the promotional literature accompanying America's interim assessments is particularly light on evidence, of any sort, that they are worth what they cost. And their costs are not trivial, either in terms of money spent or in classroom time taken.

Perhaps in the future, research evidence supporting the instructional dividends of interim assessments will be available. However, it is possible that there is an inherent but unrecognized flaw in the interim assessment approach—a flaw that dooms these tests to be ineffectual, particularly in improving instruction. Interim tests, you see, are administered at a given time during the school year, for instance, in the middle of or near the close of every three-month segment. So in order for the results of these tests to help teachers instructionally, the timing of the teacher's instruction must mesh with what's covered in a given interim test. A test covering yet untaught content, or content that was treated weeks ago, will hardly inform a teacher's decision making. Accordingly, either teachers allow the curricular pacing of their instruction to be regimented by what's to be assessed on these interim tests (and few teachers relish such regimentation) or teachers will find their instruction is out of line with what's being tested. Perhaps this is why no evidence regarding the profound payoffs of interim tests has yet been seen. Maybe, for most teachers, interim assessments just don't work.

Conclusion

Nonetheless, we continue to see ardent advocacy for the installation of balanced-assessment approaches. Much of this advocacy can be traced back to the very folks who sell such tests. If balanced assessment comes to be seen as *necessarily* including interim assessments, then those who sell such assessments can be assured of a serious slice of assessment's fiscal pie. Yet, until suitable support for interim tests arrives, balanced assessment will most definitely remain out of balance.

What We Know

- Classroom formative assessment works well, and the process can be successfully used by classroom teachers in diverse ways.
- Society now demands evidence from large-scale accountability tests to evaluate the success of tax-supported schooling.
- Interim assessments, at the moment, are supported neither by research evidence nor by a societal demand.

About the Author

W. James Popham is professor emeritus at the University of California, Los Angeles (UCLA), Graduate School of Education and Information Studies. He spent the bulk of his educational career as a schoolteacher and later taught courses in instructional methods for prospective teachers as well as courses in evaluation and measurement for graduate students at UCLA. He has written and cowritten thirty books, 200 journal articles, fifty research reports, and 175 papers.

References and Further Reading

Arter, J. A. (2010). *Interim benchmark assessments: Are we getting our eggs in the right basket?* Paper presented at the annual meeting of the National Council on Measurement in Education, Denver, CO.

Black, P., & Wiliam, D. (1998). Inside the black box: Raising standards through classroom assessment. *Phi Delta Kappan, 80,* 139–148.

Heritage, M. (2010a). *Formative assessment and next-generation assessment systems: Are we losing an opportunity?* Washington, DC: Council of Chief State School Officers.

Heritage, M. (2010b). *Formative assessment: Making it happen in the classroom.* Thousand Oaks, CA: Corwin.

Popham, W. J. (2010). *Everything school leaders need to know about assessment.* Thousand Oaks, CA: Corwin.

7

Do We Need an Assessment Overhaul?

Jay McTighe and Grant Wiggins

Jay McTighe and *Grant Wiggins* suggest a different approach to measuring students' progress.

The emergence the new Common Core State Standards presents an opportunity to reexamine the current system of educational assessments in the United States. For the past ten years, the No Child Left Behind Act of 2001 (NCLB) federal statute has required annual state testing as a means of gauging student achievement. Publishing these test scores establishes accountability, comparing schools and districts and resulting in consequences for schools that fail to achieve "annual yearly progress" quotas. Responsible educators understand the need for accountability, and the NCLB testing program has revealed achievement deficiencies that demand to be addressed. Nonetheless, the present assessment system is flawed and ironically may impede the very efforts needed to attain important educational goals.

The adage "What gets measured signals what is important" rings true in education. Students regularly ask their teachers, "Will this be on the test?" If the answer is "no," they are less likely to pay attention. Large-scale assessments naturally hold even greater sway. Teachers and administrators pay close attention to state and provincial assessments since their results can have high-stakes consequences not only for students but for schools. If something is not assessed, it can receive less emphasis in the classroom. The result is often a *de facto* narrowing of the curriculum and misguided "test prep" interventions.

Currently, NCLB employs a "snapshot" approach to assessment through annual state testing in targeted subject areas. Given the large-scale nature of these tests, the majority of them understandably employ a selected-response format, allowing for fast, inexpensive machine scoring. This type of assessment is simply incapable of measuring students' responses to open-ended problems and issues, discussion and debate, extended writing for real audiences, or showing substantive research and experimental inquiry. Moreover, many subject areas for which standards exist are not tested at all in many states, and nor do these accountability measures typically test the so-called 21st century skills of creative thinking, teamwork, multimedia communication, and use of information technologies. It can be argued that current standardized assessments fail to assess many of the most valued goals of schooling.

An Alternative Approach

We recommend an alternative approach to assessment that can minimize unhealthy curriculum narrowing, provide more robust evidence of academic knowledge and 21st century outcomes, and support meaningful learning through authentic and engaging teaching. Our framework offers a viable approach for achieving three inter-related goals:

- Assessing the most important educational goals in appropriate ways
- Providing the specific and timely feedback needed to improve learning
- Supporting curriculum planning, local assessment, and teaching for meaningful learning

To achieve these goals, we propose a "multiple measures" approach, with three components for assessing core requirements and other important educational outcomes. These are as follows:

- Content-specific tests
- A series of content-specific and interdisciplinary performance tasks
- A local assessment component

Content-Specific Tests

Content-specific tests, consisting of multiple choice and brief constructed response (BCR) items designed to test core requirements, do have a value. These types of test have been proven to be effective and efficient at sampling a broad array of basic knowledge and skills drawn from the curriculum. These tests should be computer-based in order to take advantage of enhanced item types made possible through technology-enabled assessments and to provide nearly immediate feedback in the form of detailed item analyses (not just scores).

We further propose that a matrix sampling approach be considered as a cost-saving means of obtaining accountability information at the school and district levels without subjecting every student to testing every year on every aspect of the Core Standards. However, states or school districts could opt for census testing if individual student scores are desired. Of course, this type of testing is limited, and therefore needs to be accompanied by other types of test.

Content-Specific and Interdisciplinary Performance Tasks

Performance tasks call for students to apply their learning to new situations in context. Accordingly, they are better suited to assessing more complex concepts and 21st century skills, such as mathematical reasoning, scientific investigation, issues analysis, creative problem solving, oral communications, and technology applications. Performance assessments should be set in real-world contexts and include both content-specific and interdisciplinary performances. Importantly, they should be implemented by teachers *as part of the curriculum* at designated time periods during the school year. Other nations (e.g., the United Kingdom) already include assessments scored by teachers as a major element of their national assessments.

This type of assessment would ideally be translated into a national database of performance tasks and companion scoring rubrics, accessible to all teachers so that ideas and resources can be shared. This would also be a base from which national or regional assessments could be developed.

It is important to note that scoring would not be contracted to commercial test companies, although companies may be enlisted to help with training, moderation, and reporting. Indeed, a central feature of this proposal relates to the high-impact professional development that accrues when teachers work in teams to score students' work. Accordingly, the costs of scoring the performance tasks need to be conceived and budgeted as a joint expenditure for assessment *and* professional development.

Local Assessments

Standardized national assessment systems are incapable of assessing every student on every educational goal. Therefore, the third component of our system legitimizes the role of local assessment, trusting teachers with the responsibility of scoring work in *all* subject areas. The results, framed in terms of a system of standards, would be made public.

The local component of the assessment system allows for a wide variety of possibilities, including common course exams, student projects and exhibitions, and interdisciplinary tasks involving collaboration and technology applications. More specifically, it does the following:

- Can appropriately assess important achievement targets (e.g., oral reading and speaking, applications of technology, teamwork) that may otherwise "fall through the cracks"
- Is based on local curricula so that teachers, students, and parents will be more likely to "own" the measures and the results
- Offers greater flexibility and potential for differentiation (e.g., giving students some choice of topics or products) than standardized assessments
- Honors the tradition of local control of education by allowing local decision making, rather than having all high-stakes assessments imposed from the outside
- Targets student accountability (i.e., the results become part of local grading and reporting)

A cornerstone of this third component is a Student Standards Folder—a systematic collection of assessment evidence related to Core Standards and other important educational goals. This would include the results from the performance tasks, content-specific tests, and local assessments, as well as rubrics in each subject area to enable more systematic tracking of student achievement (i.e., progress toward meeting standards). The folder would be audited on an annual basis by regional teams of educators and "citizen experts," with two content areas sampled each year for a state audit. The system would enable educators, parents, and students to track progress over time.

Conclusion

Sadly, the use of classroom time in many schools (at least in the tested grades and subjects) would lead one to conclude that the mission of schools is to improve test taking savvy and raise test scores, rather than to strive for meaningful learning. Of course, it makes sense to familiarize students with test format, but excessive test preparation is *not* the best long-term strategy for developing a well-rounded, educated person *or* improving scores on yearly accountability tests. We contend that our three-part system provides a more comprehensive system for assessment, while avoiding some of the problems of current accountability testing.

What We Know

- Current standardized assessments do not adequately assess many of the most valued goals of schooling.
- A better "multiple measures" approach would include content-specific tests, a series of content-specific and interdisciplinary performance tasks, and a local assessment component.
- This would help schools to test what they teach, rather than teaching to the test.

About the Authors

Jay McTighe is an educational consultant. With an extensive background in professional development, he is a regular speaker at national and international conferences and workshops. He has coauthored eleven books, including the best-selling *Understanding by Design* series with Grant Wiggins, and written more than thirty articles and book chapters. Jay earned his master's degree from the University of Maryland and has completed postgraduate studies at Johns Hopkins University.

Grant Wiggins is the president of Authentic Education, New Jersey. He and his colleagues organize conferences and workshops; develop print and web resources; and consult with schools, colleges, districts, and state and national education departments on a variety of reform matters on key education issues. Grant has coauthored many books and articles, and his work has been supported by the Pew Charitable Trusts, the Geraldine R. Dodge Foundation, and the National Science Foundation (NSF). Previously, he had fourteen years' experience in secondary schools, teaching electives in English and philosophy.

Reference and Further Reading

Wiggins, G., & McTighe, J. (2007). *Schooling by design: Mission, action, achievement.* Alexandria: ASCD.

8

Formative Assessment

An Enabler of Learning

Margaret Heritage

> Formative assessment can be a powerful day-to-day tool for teachers and students. **Margaret Heritage** explains.

Formative assessment is often misconstrued. Routinely, it is conceptualized as a "test" or an "instrument" that is more fine-grained and administered more frequently than other types of assessment. This formulation misses its documented power for improving student learning. When formative assessment is conceived as a practice implemented by teachers in collaboration with their students, then its promise as an enabler rather than an evaluator of learning can be realized.

The essential purpose of formative assessment as a practice is to move students' learning forward while their learning is still in the process of developing. This stands in contrast to other forms of assessment, which evaluate learning after a period of teaching. Formative assessment practice operates as a feedback loop in which both teachers and students can play active, distinctive, yet complementary roles in enabling learning by consistently working to build and consolidate student understanding and skills during the course of a lesson.

The Teacher's Role

Formative assessment is effective only when teachers are clear about the intended learning goals for a lesson. This means focusing on what students will learn, as opposed to what they will do, which is often where teachers are tempted to start. To achieve maximum transparency for students, teachers share the learning goal, or actively create it with students, at the beginning of the lesson. In addition, teachers communicate the indicators of progress toward the learning goal or determine them in collaboration with the students. These indicators serve as signposts for both teachers and students about progress during the lesson.

With clarity about the goal and indicators, teachers can then decide how they will gather evidence of emergent learning. There is no single way to collect formative evidence because formative assessment is not a specific kind of test. For example, teachers can gather evidence through interactions with students, observations of their tasks and activities, or analysis of their work products. However, there are two important points about evidence collection. First, whatever method teachers use to elicit evidence of learning, it should yield information that is actionable by them and their students. Second, evidence collection is a systematic process and needs to be planned so that teachers have a constant stream of information tied to indicators of progress. At the same time, of course, teachers will be collecting evidence on the fly—those unplanned, spontaneous moments when students do or say something that give an indication of where they are in relation to the lesson goal.

Feedback

Feedback is a crucial component of formative assessment, and it has two aspects. First, feedback obtained from planned or spontaneous evidence is an essential resource for teachers to shape new learning through adjustments in their instruction. If teachers use evidence effectively to inform their instruction, it will render previous assessment information out of date: student learning will have progressed and will need to be assessed again. Instruction can again be adjusted to make sure that learning is on track. For this reason, a constant stream of evidence from formative assessment is necessary during lessons.

Second, feedback that the teacher provides to students is also an essential resource so the students can take active steps to advance their own learning. In reality, the feedback to students can be understood as instructional action. As the extensive literature on feedback suggests, teacher feedback is most beneficial when it assists students in understanding their current learning status and provides hints, suggestions, or cues for them to act on. It is this, rather than offering general praise or total solutions, that enables students to assume a degree of responsibility for their learning.

The teacher's role also involves helping students develop the skills to make metacognitive judgments about their learning in relation to the goal being aimed for and to establish a repertoire of strategies to regulate their own learning.

The Students' Role

The students' role in formative assessment begins when they have a clear conception of the learning target. Just as the teacher is collecting evidence in relation to the goal, so, too, are the students through self-assessment—a separate but complementary feedback process. In self-assessment students engage in metacognitive activity, a hallmark of effective learning. Metacognitive activity involves students in thinking about their own learning while they are learning. In this process, they are generating internal feedback that tells them when they need to make adjustments to their learning strategies. These adjustments might include, for example, drawing a diagram to help in the understanding of a mathematical problem, or determining that more research is needed to be able to analyze historical events, or rereading a text to clarify the meaning.

The students' role ideally also includes peer assessment. In peer assessment, students give feedback to their classmates that is intended to be constructive and help them make progress toward the lesson goal. Peers assess each other's learning against the same indicators that they use to check on their own learning when they are engaged in self-assessment. Peer feedback has a number of advantages both for those students providing the feedback and for those receiving it. It involves thinking about learning and can deepen students' understanding of their own learning because they have to internalize the learning goal and progress indicators in the context of someone else's work.

The final point about the students' role in formative assessment is that they actually use the feedback. It is important that students have to both reflect on their learning and use the feedback to advance learning. One teacher summed up the changes she made to ensure that this time was preserved in her lessons: "I used to do more but now I do less. Now I work hard to save time for student reflection rather than filling every minute [of the lesson] with activity."

Overall, the feedback loop is fueled by three convergent sources of feedback: from teachers, peers, and the students themselves. However, the successful provision and use of this feedback is dependent on the nature of the classroom climate in which the learning is taking place.

Classroom Climate

An essential aspect of formative assessment is classroom climate. Three particular elements are key. First, power and responsibility in the classroom are not just the teacher's prerogative but are distributed so that teachers and students work together to share responsibility for learning. Second, the classroom has to be a safe place. Students must be able to ask for help, regard errors as sources of new learning, and admit difficulties or problems without fearing that these actions will diminish them in the eyes of their teachers or their peers. Instead, they need to know that such behaviors are desirable and are characteristic of effective learners. Finally, it means that the relationships in the classroom must be supportive and collaborative, characterized by mutual trust among teachers and students.

Conclusion

The important thing about formative assessment is that it be neither a test nor an instrument but rather an approach to teaching and learning that uses feedback as its centerpiece in a supportive classroom context. Formative assessment is a practice that empowers teachers and students to give their best to enable learning. In the end, the success of formative assessment as an enabler of learning depends on the knowledge and skills of teachers to implement this approach in collaboration with their students, not on test developers.

What We Know

- Formative assessment is not a kind of test.
- Formative assessment practice, when implemented effectively, can have powerful effects on learning.
- Formative assessment involves teachers making adjustments to their instruction based on evidence collected and providing students with feedback that helps them advance their learning.
- Students participate in the practice of formative assessment through self- and peer assessment.

About the Author

Margaret Heritage is assistant director for professional development at the National Center for Research on Evaluation, Standards and Student Testing (CRESST) at the University of California, Los Angeles (UCLA). She has written and cowritten numerous articles and books on formative assessment.

References and Further Reading

Black, P. J., & Wiliam, D. (1998). Assessment and classroom learning. *Assessment in education: Principles, Policy, & Practice, 5,* 7–73.

Hattie, J., & Timperley, H. (2007). The power of feedback. *Review of Educational Research, 77,* 81–112.

9

Upgrading High-Stakes Assessments

Albert Oosterhof

Albert Oosterhof *describes current research into the effectiveness of a new assessment strategy.*

High-stakes assessments have existed for many years; for instance, the ordinance that created the Regents Examinations in New York State was passed in 1864. The use of high-stakes assessments has become widespread in recent years, and in the United States their prevalence increased with passage of the No Child Left Behind Act of 2001 (NCLB). As the term *high stakes* suggests, students' performance on these assessments can result in significant actions directed at students, teachers, and/or schools.

Information derived from high-stakes assessments is used summatively, not formatively. Because of the large number of students involved, the assessments must be highly efficient with regard to administration and scoring. This constrains the formats that can be used and limits testing to a subset of competencies typically associated with the standards being assessed. Teachers are motivated to emphasize this subset to help their students perform well on the tests. This narrowing of the curriculum is likely to become more significant as state governments consider legislation that links school ratings and teachers' salaries to test scores. Nevertheless, by using carefully constructed performance assessments, it is possible to assess important skills that are excluded from present high-stakes tests. The problem is that, as long as these large-scale tests are administered to each student rather than samples of students, the cost to administer and score these complex assessments will be unacceptably high.

A New Assessment Strategy

Through a three-year grant from the U.S. Department of Education, the Center for Advancement of Learning and Assessment at Florida State University has been examining the feasibility of a three-pronged strategy that may do the following:

- Help expand the range of skills evaluated by statewide assessments
- Add a formative aspect to these assessments

The three components are as follows:

- *Administering performance assessments to samples of students.* The first component involves developing a series of performance assessments that measure selected state-level benchmarks and are administered to carefully selected samples of students. This part of the strategy estimates student proficiency at the group level and, like the National Assessment of Educational Progress (NAEP), is not designed to determine individual student proficiency. The content and number of performance assessments are controlled to provide appropriate generalizability, with emphasis placed on competencies that cannot be effectively measured using conventional assessments. Using sampling would be less expensive than testing every student.
- *Assessing each individual student.* The second component focuses on the proficiency in complex skills of each individual student. It entails developing performance assessment "specifications" that define comparable measures to be developed by teachers, linking teachers' assessments to those administered statewide to samples of students. Students' performance levels on the teachers' summative assessments are then compared to performance on the assessments administered statewide to samples of students. Assessments administered to these samples substantiate the reasonableness of student outcomes observed through the assessments of teachers and vice versa.
- *Using performance assessments formatively.* To be effective, these expanded assessment procedures must facilitate learning rather than increase the burdens placed on teachers and school administrators. The third component, therefore, involves using the performance assessments not just summatively but also formatively as an integral part of instruction. Results on performance-based measures would provide the basis for formative feedback to students throughout the school year. Feedback would also link performance on the task to the broader set of tasks implicit in the performance assessment specification. Teachers' performance assessments eventually have a summative role, establishing what individual students have learned. However, at the classroom and school levels, the major focus is on their formative role. We will employ what research has identified as "best practices" related to the use of formative feedback to students.

Our Research Strategy

Our research is simulating the previously stated components in a controlled setting. We are producing and administering the external assessments that ultimately would be developed by a state assessment office. These assessments are then administered to students enrolled in participating classrooms, not statewide to samples of students. We know that a NAEP-type approach can estimate achievement of groups of students from samples. What we do not know is whether separate external- and teacher-developed performance assessments, based on common specifications, can validate each other and help substantiate teachers' summative assessments of individual students.

Our present research occurs in the context of science instruction taught at the middle school level. The intent, however, is to establish procedures that are useful at other grade levels and in other subject areas. To maximize the benefits of the research, we believe teachers and school administrators must assume ownership of the ideas and procedures that evolve. Therefore, we use a partnering relationship between teachers, curriculum specialists, measurement experts, and training specialists.

Measuring Cognitive Processes

When using authentic performance assessments, it is tempting to assume that we are directly measuring the intended outcomes of learning. Any assessment, however, involves measuring something that cannot be seen—that is, a student's cognitive processes. The performance of a student is only an *indicator* of what the student knows and is thinking.

Knowledge exists at different levels of complexity. Also, different types of performance provide better indicators of different categories of knowledge. We have used categories of knowledge based on those often used in cognitive psychology:

- *Declarative knowledge:* Being able to explain things, such as how distillation works
- *Procedural knowledge:* Being able to invoke learned techniques, often in new applications, such as using distillation to separate compounds
- *Problem solving:* Having a goal but not yet identifying a means for reaching it. Problem solving uses strategies that rely on declarative and procedural knowledge, such as recognizing whether distillation can help identify the presence of a particular chemical in a solution.

We are particularly interested in complex skills that cannot be assessed with conventional tests and have found it easier to address complexity levels after identifying the focus of a particular assessment using the above categories of knowledge. For instance, a performance assessment involving procedural knowledge might ask a pupil to accurately determine true north, east, south, and west using sun shadows, without reference to other objects that indicate direction. A conventional test would involve a less complex task, as illustrated with this multiple-choice item:

A stake has been placed straight up, on flat ground, in sunlight. When does the stake's shadow fall in a true north and south direction?

A. When the shadow is at its shortest length (correct)
B. When the end of the shadow is moving the fastest (incorrect)

With declarative knowledge, a performance assessment might ask a pupil to explain in writing (1) what you did to find true north, east, south, and west and (2) why your technique works. A less complex declarative task would be presented with this multiple-choice item:

At any location in the United States, when does "local noon" occur?

   A. When the sun is exactly south of that location (correct)
   B. When the local time zone switches from morning to afternoon (incorrect)

Our Research Findings

Two science teachers and their students from each of five middle schools are participating in the research. Ten specifications were developed to define performance assessments, each designed to measure a complex competency. Two of the competencies being used are as follows:

- Formulate a scientifically testable question that relates to the context or data provided.
- Observe and describe a local ecosystem and determine potential limiting factors for specified populations in the ecosystem

Teachers and researchers independently developed, administered, and scored performance assessments based on the same specifications. Because of practical constraints, teachers at each school were limited to working with four of the ten specifications. Students completed both the teachers' and corresponding researchers' assessments. Teachers at a given school scored each other's assessments, with the median correlation between teachers' scores being 0.82. Pairs of raters similarly scored each assessment developed by researchers, with the median correlation being 0.89. In most cases, assessments developed by teachers and researchers resulted in similar score distributions. This suggests that teacher and external assessments under prescribed conditions have the potential to help validate each other and to help substantiate the teachers' summative assessments of their students.

Teachers also identified enabling competencies and used formative assessments designed to help their students achieve the more complex competencies associated with the respective specifications. Significant training and mentoring are required to optimize this formative component.

Important Issues to Be Addressed

Our research has yet to address some important issues related to upgrading high-stakes assessments. For instance, any written test or performance assessment involves only a sample of tasks that might have been used for the assessment. An important question is whether the same conclusions regarding student achievement would have been reached had different, equally appropriate tasks been used. If students' performance does not "generalize," the assessment is of limited value because conclusions based on performance depend on what task was sampled. Generalizability of high-stakes assessments must be high and involve facets *in addition to tasks* (e.g., samples of raters used to score performance).

The validity of an assessment is a critical issue. Assessments always involve indicators—not direct observation—of knowledge. Validation means establishing a link between the knowledge we seek to assess and the tasks we ask students to complete. Similarly, interpretation of performance requires establishing this link in the opposite direction between what students were observed doing and the knowledge being assessed. Evidence-centered design provides a possible framework for accomplishing this task.

Scalability and practicality are also important issues that must be resolved if we are to successfully implement this alternative approach to high-stakes assessment programs.

Notification Required by Funding Agency

This research is supported through a grant from Education Research Programs at the Institute of Education Sciences (IES), award number R305A110121, administered by the U.S. Department of Education. Faranak Rohani, director of the Center for Advancement of Learning and Assessment, is the principal investigator for this research. Related information is available at http://cala.fsu.edu/ies/. Findings and opinions do not reflect the positions or policies of the IES or the U.S. Department of Education.

What We Know

- If assessments de-emphasize particular types of competencies, what students learn will reflect this change. For practical reasons, high-stakes tests de-emphasize complex skills. It may be practical to assess these skills if samples of students are used.
- Because tests involve only samples of tasks, students' performance may not generalize to what would have been observed had different, equally appropriate tasks been used. Further research related to generalizability is required.

About the Author

Albert Oosterhof is professor emeritus in educational psychology and learning systems at Florida State University and a research associate at the university's Center for Advancement of Learning and Assessment. The focus of his work is on student assessment.

References and Further Reading

Chi, M. T. H., & Ohlsson, S. (2005). Complex declarative learning. In K. J. Holyoak & R. G. Morrison (Eds.), *Cambridge handbook of thinking and reasoning* (pp. 371–399). New York: Cambridge University Press.

Mislevy, R. J., Almond, R. G., & Lukas, J. F. (2004). *A brief introduction to evidence-centered design* (CSE Report 632). Los Angeles: University of California, National Center for Research on Evaluation, Standards, and Student Testing. Retrieved from www.cse.ucla.edu/products/reports/r632.pdf

Oosterhof, A., Rohani, F., Sanfilippo, C., Stillwell, P., & Hawkins, K. (2008). *The capabilities-complexity model.* Symposium paper presented at the National Conference on Student Assessment, Orlando, FL. Retrieved from www.cala.fsu.edu/files/ccm.pdf

Solano-Flores, G., Shavelson, R. J., Ruiz-Promo, M. A., Schultz, S. E., & Wiley, E. W. (1997). *On the development and scoring of classification and observation science performance assessments* (CSE Technical Report 458). Los Angeles: University of California, National Center for Research on Evaluation, Standards, and Student Testing. Retrieved from www.cse.ucla.edu/products/reports/TECH458.pdf

England Versus Wales

Education Performance and Accountability

Sandra McNally

*There is increasing disparity between the achievement of students in England and Wales. **Sandra McNally** explores the possible causes.*

In many respects, the education systems in England and Wales are very similar. They had a shared history within the United Kingdom until Welsh devolution in 1999, and although differences have increased since then, the main examination for sixteen-year-olds in both countries remains the General Certificate of Secondary Education (GCSE), which awards academic qualifications to students in specific subjects. GCSEs are graded from A* (pronounced as "A star") to G. In the United Kingdom, examinations at sixteen are a key educational milestone.

In this chapter, we consider a few of the differences between education in England and Wales—focusing on accountability in particular. We discuss possible reasons for the difference in educational performance and the potential contribution of differing policies on the publication of "league tables" of examination results.

Comparing Educational Performance in England and Wales

Looking at GCSE attainment in England and Wales, it is interesting to observe that the two countries used to perform exactly the same in terms of national statistics (at least between 1998 and 2001), with differences starting to emerge from 2002 onward—escalating after 2004. Figure 10.1 shows the headline statistic in the two countries.

England and Wales also used to have similar assessments for students at the end of primary (elementary) school, and the results are comparable up to about the year

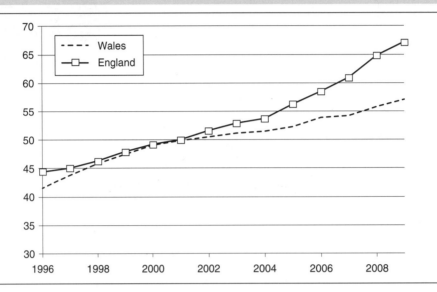

Figure 10.1   Percentage of Students Achieving Five or More GCSEs With a Grade of A* to C

2000. In this case, the two countries also performed similarly in the mid-1990s (particularly for English), with a divergence emerging in 1998 (for English) and 1999 (for math)—and England taking over.

Are "League Tables" Responsible?

League tables are produced annually by the U.K. Government's Department for Education and currently list statistics for GCSE exam performance by every school in England, as well as several other key indicators. Previously, the tables also included information for Wales, but this was scrapped by the Welsh Assembly in 2001. This coincides with the date when England and Wales began to diverge in terms of GCSE grades.

League tables continue as a prominent feature of education in England. The rationale is that they provide information to parents on the relative performance of different schools, and that parents can use this information to help them decide where to send their children. Although league tables report more than just raw exam grades, qualitative evidence suggests that school principals focus almost exclusively on the previously reported indicator (five or more "good grades"). Also, quantitative research suggests that raw grades are important in terms of the premium paid on house prices for living near a "good school."

Could the abolition of league tables in Wales somehow be responsible for this diverging performance with England? And what would this mean? First take the case where we really believe the GCSE indicator is an accurate measure of how much knowledge and skills students acquire at school. Then the divergence with England is most definitely a bad thing, and the abolition of league tables in Wales could be responsible to the extent that school principals stop making such an effort because outcomes are less visible.

Funding and Policy Differences

On the other hand, there are other things that might explain the divergence. For example, it is well known that average funding per student is much lower in Wales. Currently, funding per student is about 10 percent lower in Wales than in England.

Furthermore, many policy initiatives introduced in England have not been introduced in Wales since devolution. It is not clear *a priori* whether this is a good or a bad thing. However, some policies have been properly evaluated. One of the big differences between England and Wales is that the national literacy and numeracy strategies that were introduced in England in the late 1990s were not introduced in Wales. The strategies involved England adopting a very centralized approach toward literacy and numeracy hours that had to be implemented in primary schools. These were quite prescriptive in terms of the pedagogy. Policy makers in Wales rejected the "top-down" approach and instead encouraged local authorities and schools to develop their own locally based initiatives. Research evidence shows that diverging attainment at age eleven between England and Wales is associated with the introduction of the strategies in England, even when taking account of other school-level characteristics. The first cohorts exposed to the literacy and numeracy strategies in England would have taken their GCSE examinations in 2003 and 2004, respectively. It is around this time that the divergence between England and Wales really starts to escalate.

There is only so much one can infer from looking at trends in raw results between countries. There are at least three competing explanations for the apparent deterioration in Wales—the abolition of league tables, lower per-student funding, and the decision not to implement national literacy and numeracy strategies in Wales.

Are High-Stakes Tests the Best Measure of Student Knowledge?

Another question is whether the divergence between England and Wales after 2001 in GCSE attainment really reflects differences in the extent to which students have appropriated knowledge and skills. It is often argued that "high-stakes" tests encourage various teacher practices designed to boost results, but not necessarily knowledge and skills. These practices include the following:

- Coaching students to respond to test questions rather than teaching them mastery of a subject
- Narrowing their focus to cover only those topics that will be assessed
- Focusing on students near the threshold of the headline indicator at the expense of other students
- Encouraging students to take "easy" subjects
- Outright cheating (sometimes) (e.g., misuse of continuous assessment)

There have been many international studies that find evidence of these practices in cases where high-stakes testing is introduced. One of the ways this is shown is by comparing results in high-stakes tests versus low-stakes tests for the same students. It has often been found that the improvement in high-stakes tests (like GCSE) is not reflected in low-stakes tests. Such considerations have led to recommendations that education authorities separate assessments that aim to measure educational progress from assessments that aim to incentivize schools and teachers. (This is a recommendation of Professor Derek Neal of the University of Chicago, who has recently produced a review of evidence on the design of performance pay in education.)

It is plausible that at least some of the relative deterioration in performance in Wales compared to England came about because the relative incentive to engage in such practices was diminished in Wales.

However, there is a low-stakes test to which we might refer. Both England and Wales participated in the Organisation for Economic Co-operation and Development (OECD) international test for fifteen-year-olds (Programme for International Student Assessment [PISA]) in 2006 and 2009. This could be thought of as low stakes because school performance in PISA is not made publicly available. In both years, average performance in Wales was lower than that in England. Furthermore, comparing 2006 and 2009, performance decreased in reading, mathematics, and science in Wales whereas there was little change in England. This suggests the increasing gap between England and Wales is not just an artifact of the British examination system or the incentives produced by differing policies about league tables. One might debate the extent of the difference, but the existence of the phenomenon seems to be well founded. Possible reasons merit further investigation.

What We Know

- Educational performance has lowered in Wales compared to England in recent years.
- The timing coincides with the scrapping of publication of exam results in Wales.
- Other potential explanations are lower funding per student in Wales and the success of the literacy and numeracy strategies in England.
- The abolition of "league tables" of examination results in Wales gave teachers less incentive to focus narrowly on assessment. A recent paper by Burgess, Wilson, and Worth (2010) suggests that this had a negative impact on school performance.
- International low-stakes tests also suggest a relative decline in Wales.

About the Author

Sandra McNally is a professor of economics at the University of Surrey. She is also director of the Education and Skills Programme at the Centre for Economic Performance, London School of Economics.

References and Further Reading

BBC News. (2010, December 7). *PISA tests show students in Wales falling further behind*. Retrieved from www.bbc.co.uk/news/uk-wales-11930257

Bradshaw, J., Ager, R., Burge, B., & Wheater, R. (2010). *PISA 2009 achievement of 15-year-olds in England*. Slough, UK: National Foundation for Educational Research.

Burgess, S., Wilson, D., & Worth, J. (2010). *A natural experiment in school accountability: The impact of school performance information on pupil progress and sorting*. (CMPO Working Paper No. 10/246). Bristol, UK: University of Bristol.

Gibbons, S., Machin, S., & Silva, O. (2009). *Valuing school quality using boundary discontinuity regression* (SERC Discussion Paper 18). London: London School of Economics.

Machin, S., & McNally, S. (2009). *The three Rs: What scope is there for literacy and numeracy policies to raise pupil achievement?* London: Centre for Economic Performance, London School of Economics.

Neal, D. (2011, January). *The design of performance pay in education* (National Bureau of Economic Research Working Paper No. 16710). Retrieved from http://www.nber.org/papers/w16710

Wilson, D., Croxson, B., & Atkinson, A. (2006). What gets measured gets done. *Policy Studies, 27*(2), 153–171.

In Search of Feasible Fidelity

David Andrews

*When deciding whether to adopt an evidence-based approach, educators should weigh the costs and benefits, explains **David Andrews,** and be prepared to implement it with fidelity.*

Educators who remain unaware of the need to make data-driven decisions and adopt evidence-based practices to improve student learning either live in severe isolation or choose to ignore the call. The call for the use of data-driven decisions and the implementation of evidence-based practices in education permeates universities, government agencies, professional associations, and both the nonprofit and for-profit sectors of education.

The consistent message regarding the importance of using data to improve student outcomes has led to a noted increase in formal testing (summative assessments) and associated accountability measures in schools. There are also promising increases in ongoing assessments (formative) solely used to improve the day-to-day educational experiences of students. Nonetheless, the growth of implementing our most scientifically proven, evidence-based approaches continues to lag behind other efforts to use data in making educational decisions.

Educational researchers are working diligently to develop, scientifically evaluate, and refine evidence-based approaches to maximize student learning. The result is a growing list of evidence-based approaches, which are described and documented in repositories like the Best Evidence Encyclopedia (BEE) website (www.bestevidence .org). Given that most educators are passionate about student learning, one might assume that teachers and their principals queue up in droves to implement the most evidence-based strategies and programs. Intuitively, educators worthy of their chalk would clamor to use "what works." In reality, the movement toward sustained adoption of evidence-based approaches cannot be described as a stampede toward better outcomes.

One reason for the slow, and perhaps inexplicable, reluctance to adopt evidence-based approaches is an incomplete understanding of what is required to adopt and implement these approaches with fidelity. Fidelity means implementing the approach exactly as it was developed and tested. Without fidelity, there are no assurances that expected outcomes will be achieved.

Adopting and implementing an evidence-based approach requires faith in the presented evidence, followed by a commitment to the appropriate implementation fidelity. Understanding the depth of the commitment required will determine whether or not the approach "works" in specific settings for specific educators and their students. Consequently, educators must evaluate the feasibility of the fidelity that is required to get the desired outcome. This may appear a daunting task, but it can be approached systematically in a series of considerations for choosing and sustaining a specific evidence-based approach.

Choosing to Adopt

The choice to adopt an evidence-based approach begins with a cost-benefit analysis. A series of questions should be asked by anyone considering adoption, and these are included in the Table 11.1.

Some costs and benefits are direct, and some are indirect. Cost includes everything that is required to get a positive outcome. Typical and obvious direct costs are related to materials, training, and personnel. These costs are easy to estimate and are usually available from those who market a given evidence-based opportunity. There are, however, other less-direct costs associated with implementing any new approach. These less-direct costs include time commitments, cost to culture and climate, and various unanticipated supports. Educators who are considering whether or not a specific evidence-based approach "will work" for their situation must be aware of both the direct and indirect costs associated with adoption. Failing to understand and commit to the entire cost (direct and indirect) puts the fidelity of implementation at risk and negates any claims that the approach is evidence based.

Analysis of the benefits of a specific evidence-based approach should always begin with a complete understanding of the expected impact on student learning. Potential adopters should demand more than just statistically significant evidence that a strategy "works." Educators must explore the practical significance of a given approach in terms of actual gains that can be expected. For example, how many children can be expected to be reading at grade level within a specific time period, given the high-fidelity implementation of a specific literacy approach?

In addition, it is important to understand other benefits that can be expected from the adoption of a specific approach. Two substantial considerations are (a) the overall impact on nonacademic factors (like attendance and discipline) that predict academic performance, and (b) the overall impact on the amount of available instructional time. Educators will be likely to note that the impact of a specific approach on the amount of instructional time available in a given day can be positive or negative.

Table II.I   Cost–Benefit Analysis Questions

Direct	Indirect
Cost	
How much do the materials cost, and do they duplicate other materials that need to be purchased?	How much teaching time will be required from personnel and pupils?
How much does the training and ongoing support cost? How much time will it require?	How much time will be expended in gaining teacher and staff support?
Will there be a need for additional personnel?	How much prep time should teachers expect outside the classroom?
Are there future hiring decisions related to staff skills that will have a fiscal impact?	What are the hidden costs in ongoing support, adoption of prerequisite programs, support for struggling staff, etc.?
What is the cost of the new technology or equipment required to implement the approach?	How much political capital will be expended in changing to a new approach?
Benefit	
What are the actual academic gains that can be expected? Are these gains practically significant in addition to being "statistically significant"?	What are the expected improvements in staff climate and morale?
What are the direct savings of teaching time associated with implementation?	What are the expected benefits from the general skill development of teachers?
What are the direct savings associated with staffing?	What are the expected benefits for leadership development?

Some benefits are even less direct and cannot be assessed until a longer period of time has passed. Increased staff retention rates due to improved job satisfaction are more difficult to assess than increased student scores on standardized tests. Nonetheless, retention of high-quality teachers is essential to the success of longer-term reform, and improvements in these rates as a result of implementing a specific practice should be explored.

A cost-benefit analysis can be completed by simply comparing the list of costs to the list of benefits. Sophisticated methods of weighting the costs and benefits could be constructed but are probably not necessary. Rather, educators should qualitatively compare the two lists and determine which warrants action. When benefits outweigh the costs, adoption should follow. If unclear patterns emerge from the cost-benefit analysis, the approach being considered might well be avoided.

Sustaining Adoption

Sustaining adoption of an evidence-based approach is as important as the decision to adopt and the initial implementation. Furthermore, sustaining the adoption can be more difficult than choosing and getting started. Initial adoption is sometimes accompanied by the excitement of innovation and the motivational energy associated with the novelty. As the novelty wears off, educators must be cognizant of the demands of sustaining the approach.

Plans for adopting an evidence-based approach should include a plan for sustaining the approach. How will the continuation funds be generated? How will new personnel be trained and assimilated into the approach? Will there be costs associated with upgrading to newer versions of the approach? All of these questions should be addressed in the sustainability plan.

It is also important to provide enough implementation time to get the expected results. Educators can be impatient—especially when the stakes are high. Some approaches take time to be implemented with the appropriate fidelity. Others have an inherent delay in the timeline for getting results (e.g., a focus on graduation with seventh graders will not yield pure outcome results for up to six years). Realistic timelines should be articulated such that evidence-based programs are given enough time to demonstrate that they are achieving the desired impact.

Sustaining programs can also be achieved by celebrating "early wins." Educators are more likely to sustain a given effort if they can see the immediate benefits of the effort. Sometimes it is necessary to be creative in identifying early wins so that educators do not lose their excitement and commitment to a specific approach. If educators do lose their enthusiasm, a booster session of training or some other incentive may be necessary to reinvigorate implementation.

Whether adopting or sustaining an evidence-based approach, the key to success is constantly promoting and celebrating feasible fidelity. If the fidelity requirements of a given approach are not feasible, there is little likelihood that the approach will have the desired impact.

What We Know

- Evidence-based approaches are not being widely adopted in classrooms.
- A cost-benefit analysis should be the starting point when deciding whether to adopt an evidence-based approach.
- Adopting and implementing an evidence-based approach requires faith in the evidence and an ongoing commitment to delivering it with fidelity.
- Teachers' enthusiasm must be maintained.

Author's Note

This article is an adaptation of the speech given by David Andrews at the Institute for Effective Education (University of York, U.K.) inaugural conference in 2011.

About the Author

David Andrews is dean of the Johns Hopkins University School of Education and was the founding dean of The Ohio State University's College of Education and Human Ecology. Throughout his career, he has been committed to improving academic and behavioral outcomes for at-risk children and young people.

Before Choosing,
Ask Three Questions

Steve Fleischman

Steve Fleischman explains the difficulties in making use of research and offers some guidance.

The Federal Trade Commission (FTC) made news in September 2011 by fining Reebok $25 million for making unsupported claims regarding its EasyTone line of athletic shoes. According to the United Kingdom's *Telegraph* newspaper, "Fitness and toning shoes have been claiming to work leg-sculpting miracles for several years now." However, the FTC found these claims to be unsubstantiated. Reebok may no longer assert that the shoes tone leg muscles or produce firmer, shapelier buttocks. As David Vladeck, the director of the FTC's Bureau of Consumer Protection stated, "Consumers expect to get a workout, not to get worked over."

Unfortunately, as educators we are all too familiar with claims that turn out to be too good to be true. Take the concept of "learning styles." Perhaps you have used the concept to guide your classroom instruction? After all, the concept and practice have been widely shared for nearly two decades. Yet you may be surprised to learn the conclusion reached in December 2008 by experts who reviewed the research literature on the subject and found "at present, there is no adequate evidence base to justify incorporating learning-styles assessments into general educational practice." The team wrote the following:

[We] found virtually no evidence . . . validating the educational applications of learning styles. Although the literature on learning styles is enormous, very few studies have even used an experimental methodology capable of testing the validity of learning styles applied to education. Moreover, of those that did use an appropriate method, several found results that flatly contradict the popular . . . hypothesis. (Pashler, McDaniel, Rohrer, & Bjork, 2009, p. 105)

The review cautioned against the practice until better evidence is provided. However, this has not stopped publishers and developers from making large amounts of money in promoting the use of "learning styles" in schools.

The flood of claims regarding effectiveness is likely to grow, given the widespread implementation of Common Core State Standards in the United States, greater emphasis on professional development and other approaches that increase educator effectiveness, and the expanded focus on online or technology based learning programs and products.

Thus, while educators may now be protected when it comes to which shoes they wear to tone their muscles, they still have little protection against choosing to use what may be ineffective programs or practices in their classrooms, schools, and districts.

Why Is Choice So Difficult?

Experts in the field note that making choices is a complex, challenging, and often irrational process. In *The Art of Choosing*, Sheena Iyengar (2010), a business professor at New York's Columbia University, points to psychological, sociological, and cultural factors that shape views, attitudes, and actions related to choice. She cites examples demonstrating that in blind tests of products such as water or wine, novices often fail to distinguish the most expensive or "best" from the rest. As Iyengar points out, "Most of us need to rely on external information in order to choose well."

In another example, Iyengar reports on an experiment she conducted that demonstrates that "too much" choice can lead to confusion and a decrease in choice making. With the cooperation of a large supermarket, she set up a booth that at different times offered tastings of either twenty-four or six of the jams produced by Wilkin & Sons. Customers who tasted the jams received a coupon allowing them to purchase their preference at a discount. Iyengar reports that "30% of the people who had seen the small assortment decided to buy jam, but only 3% bought a jar after seeing the large assortment." Thus, having more choice can inhibit choice!

It may be that too much information may be as bad as too little when making choices. And, as Chip and Dan Heath (2013) demonstrate in their book *Decisive: How to Make Better Choices in Life and Work*, we are all challenged by numerous personal biases that make effective decision making difficult. Clearly, educators need help when making decisions that may impact students for the rest of their lives.

What Type of Information Do "Education Consumers" Want?

If making choices is a difficult process, which often requires outside guidance, then what type of help would education decision makers like to receive? My colleagues at Education Northwest explored this question in a 2009 study on evidence use in education (Nelson, Leffler, & Hansen, 2009). They reported a wide gulf between research design and "real world" practice, which often results in findings with limited applicability. Furthermore, they found that educators struggle to acquire, interpret, or apply research because of their own lack of knowledge, skills, and time.

Despite these challenges, the study points to three principles that, if followed, might support improved use of evidence in education:

1. *Research should be contextualized.* Participants expressed strong preferences for research evidence linked to local contexts. Educators want to know, will this program work in my school? Will it help my students? Providing more context in a study, and its findings, helps educators answer these and similar questions.

2. *Research should be easy to read, absorb, and apply.* Participants asked that research evidence be presented in brief reports, written in nontechnical language. If researchers fail to heed this advice, even the most well-conducted study might wind up serving merely to raise the height of a computer monitor rather than the performance of students.

3. *Research should be "translated" and "transmitted" by intermediaries.* Participants defined intermediaries as trusted organizations and individuals that help to locate, sort, and prioritize available evidence. As with most aspects of life, we take advice from those we know and trust and who know best how to frame information so that it is useful to us.

Evidence Isn't Everything: Three Critical Questions

The past decade has seen an increase of evidence in education. Today, "consumer-reporting" initiatives such as the Best Evidence Encyclopedia (BEE) (United Kingdom and United States), EPPI-Centre (United Kingdom), and What Works Clearinghouse (United States) provide evidence reviews of leading programs and practices. However, having better evidence is not enough. Ultimately, we must become more sophisticated consumers of information.

My experience as a teacher, researcher, and technical assistance provider has convinced me that making sound choices in education depends on asking three fundamental questions consistently:

- *What works?* Our actions should be guided by the principle that the best approaches to use in education are those that are most likely to get the desired results. Asking this question compels us to reject opinion, ideology, marketing, and popularity and instead ask whether the proposed educational approach works. Improvement approaches should not simply sound good but rather should work well.

- *How do you know?* In the United States it is rare to encounter an education program or practice that does not claim to be "research based." This means that the provider claims that research was considered in the design of the program. However, we must go beyond these claims and, in a spirit of healthy skepticism, demand the compelling evidence that a program works. This means we must ask whether the program is "research proven" and not just "research based." The "consumer-reporting" initiatives mentioned before can provide support in answering this question.

- *So what?* This question is focused on significance. It suggests a series of critical questions that go beyond looking for generalized demonstrations of the effectiveness of a program or practice. Questions of this type include the following: Will the program be effective with my students or work in my context? Given the level of demonstrated effectiveness, is this program or practice worth the resources required to adopt and implement it? Are there better alternatives? What kind of help will I receive so that this program gets the same effects in my setting as it has elsewhere?

Iyengar (2010) concludes her book by observing the following: "Science can assist us in becoming more skillful choosers, but at its core, choice remains an art." As with all else in education, the best results for students will emerge when educators combine the best available evidence with keenly honed professional insights and judgments and a set of questions that help them to avoid their own decision-making biases.

What We Know

- Making choices is a complex and challenging process.
- Providing educators with reliable and useful evidence can support effective choices.
- Sound judgment, driven by critical questions, can improve decision making.

About the Author

Steve Fleischman is chief executive officer of Education Northwest, a nonprofit organization based in Portland, Oregon. The organization conducts research, evaluation, professional development, technical assistance, training, and strategic communications activities to promote evidence-informed education policy and practice.

References and Further Reading

Heath, C., & Heath, D. (2013). *Decisive: How to make better choices in life and work.* New York: Crown Business.

Iyengar, S. (2010). *The art of choosing.* New York: Hachette Book Group.

Lockwood, A. T., & Fleischman, S. (2010). Choosing a school turnaround provider. *Lessons Learned, 1*(3), 1–4. Portland, OR: Education Northwest. Retrieved from http://educationnorthwest.org/resource/1294

Martin, A., & O'Connor, A. (2011, September 28). Reebok to pay settlement over health claims. *New York Times*. Retrieved from http://www.nytimes.com/2011/09/29/business/reebok-to-pay-in-settlement-over-health-claims.html

Nelson, S. R., Leffler, J. C., & Hansen, B.A. (2009). *Toward a research agenda for understanding and improving the use of research evidence*. Portland, OR: Northwest Regional Educational Laboratory. Retrieved from http://educationnorthwest.org/resource/694

Pashler, H., McDaniel, M., Rohrer, D., & Bjork, R. (2009). Learning styles: Concepts and evidence. *Psychological Science in the Public Interest, 9*(3), 105–119.

Warburton, S. (2011, September 28). Reebok fined $25 million for 'toning shoes' false claims. *Telegraph*. Retrieved from http://fashion.telegraph.co.uk/article/TMG8794981/Reebok-fined-25-million-for-toning-shoes-false-claims.html

What Works in Classroom Management

Thomas Kratochwill, Rachel DeRoos, and Samantha Blair

Thomas Kratochwill, Rachel DeRoos, and Samantha Blair provide an overview of some successful approaches developed by researchers.

Classroom management, often called classroom discipline, is one of the most serious obstacles to promoting effective teaching. It has been cited as one of the most prevalent reasons for job burnout and attrition of first-year teachers, and teachers' concerns over their own safety directly relate to the use of effective classroom management programs. Students have also reported that they feel unsafe due to a lack of effective disciplinary procedures and the potential for violence.

According to Evertson and Weinstein (2006), classroom management has two distinct purposes: "It not only seeks to establish and sustain an orderly environment so students can engage in meaningful academic learning, it also aims to enhance student social and moral growth." The authors identify five specific tasks that extend beyond some of the more traditional behavior management techniques. Specifically, they note that teachers should do the following:

- Develop caring, supportive relationships with and among students.
- Organize and implement instruction in ways that optimize students' access to learning.
- Use group management methods that encourage student engagement with academic tasks.
- Promote the development of students' social skills and self-regulation.
- Use appropriate interventions to assist students who have behavior problems.

Teachers concerned with classroom management typically need help with two major issues: preventing discipline problems and dealing with current discipline problems. Prevention of classroom behavior problems is critical. To address these concerns, researchers have established several systems. One is called positive behavior support (PBS) and the other social and emotional learning (SEL). PBS programs typically involve a schoolwide structure of support for teachers who adopt evidence-based programs, and small-group and individualized programs for more serious student discipline concerns. PBS is typically set up as a multilevel or tiered model of intervention and these tiers are designed to address classroom-wide support (Tier 1), small-group support (Tier 2), and/or individual student support (Tier 3). It begins with the following:

- *Schoolwide systems of support (called universal or primary prevention; Tier 1).* Interventions at this level are applied to all students in the school. All students are instructed on the behavioral expectations for the school. Approximately 80 percent of students may respond to this level of intervention.
- *Small-group or more focused interventions (called selected or secondary intervention; Tier 2) for students who have similar problems, such as aggression.* After the primary level of prevention is applied, approximately 10 percent to 20 percent of students will need this additional level of support.
- *Individualized interventions (called indicated or tertiary intervention; Tier 3) for students who need very focused and more intense services for problematic and disruptive behavior.* Tertiary interventions are typically used with students who have a more severe range of disruptive behaviors and are directed by a collaborative team composed of teachers, parents, and staff trained in behavior management. These interventions begin with a functional assessment of the problematic behaviors, and progress is monitored throughout. Approximately 5 percent to 7 percent of students will need this level of support.

In contrast to PBS, which is based on a multitiered risk model of prevention, SEL focuses on building life skills and social competence, which works to prevent potential behavior problems and support mental health (see the article by Bear in the *Handbook of Classroom Management* [Emmer & Sabornie, 2015] for a review).

As an example of establishing social and emotional skills in the classroom, a teacher may hold class meetings or "sharing circles" in which students are encouraged to share their thoughts and feelings about school and community activities. These activities promote social interactions and build a sense of community in the classroom.

Why Classroom Management Works

Effective classroom management principles appear to work across a number of subject areas and grade levels. They work best when at least three basic principles are embedded in the practices:

- Emphasize student expectations for behavior and learning rather than focusing only on problematic behavior and discipline problems.
- Support the learning environment by promoting active learning and student involvement and not just compliance with rules.
- Identify student behaviors that are an integral part of the instructional agenda—more specifically the following:
  - What behaviors are required for the goals of the learning activities to be reached?
  - What does a particular learning activity imply about student roles?
  - How will the teacher prepare students to enact these roles successfully?

To these important recommendations, we would add that a support system (such as PBS) needs to be established so that different levels of problematic behavior can be addressed.

Effectiveness of Classroom Management Practices

Classroom management systems will be effective in the majority of classrooms, although there may be some variations when taking into account different subject areas and contextual factors. There are some important considerations related to the effectiveness of classroom management practices.

Effective classroom management must be aligned with instructional goals and activities. When teachers identify what good student behavior looks like, they can work backward from the desired outcomes to determine which management systems will be most effective. Examples of these behavioral outcomes include arriving in class and being in one's seat on time, being prepared for a lesson, paying attention, volunteering information and responding to questions, and completing assignments. Accepted behaviors may vary for different classroom organizational systems (whole-class, small-group, or individual tutoring). Classroom management strategies may need to be adapted for unique contexts and environments that emerge in typical classrooms.

Many of the most effective classroom management procedures—especially those targeting the most disruptive student behaviors—involve behavior modification and applied behavior analysis (ABA) procedures. Research has repeatedly shown these procedures to be effective across all ages and grades. They are also effective with a wide range of problematic behavior in both regular and special education classroom settings. The procedures typically involve the use of positive reinforcement, negative reinforcement, and time-out interventions.

Timing

Research suggests that beginning-of-the-year activities are extremely important for effective classroom management systems. Within the first few days and weeks of the start of a school year, an effective classroom management system should be fully in place. However, an individual program for disruptive behavior can be established at any time.

Once a classroom management system is established, the system should be applied throughout the year and across grades so that students receive constant and consistent messages about classroom expectations, rules, and procedures. This strategy will ensure that positive student behavior is supported and reinforced throughout the year.

Developmental Differences

Although the majority of classroom management research has focused on elementary school classrooms, with little research devoted to secondary levels, the basic principles can be applied across all grades.

At the secondary level, some teacher responsibility for classroom management can be shifted to administrators who may invoke disciplinary sanctions or procedures. In terms of further developmental differences, an important dimension of classroom management is starting out on the "right foot." Emmer, Evertson, and Anderson (1980), who conducted a study in twenty-eight third-grade classrooms, found that effective classroom managers consistently demonstrated three behaviors:

- *Conveying purposefulness.* Teachers maximize the use of available time for instruction to emphasize student learning and not just classroom behavior.
- *Teaching students appropriate conduct.* Effective teachers were clear about what they expected and what they would not tolerate.
- *Maintaining students' attention.* Effective teachers continuously monitored students for confusion and inattention and were sensitive to student concerns.

Evertson and Emmer (1982) reported similar results but with a few unique findings. Middle school teachers reported that they did not spend as much time teaching students to follow rules and procedures. Nevertheless, they needed to communicate expectations related to engaging in and completing work assignments. The authors listed the following characteristics of effective classroom managers at the middle school level:

- *Instructing students in rules and procedures.* Effective classroom managers described rules completely and systematically instilled the rules and procedures.
- *Monitoring student compliance with rules.* The best classroom managers monitored compliance and consistently intervened to correct inappropriate behavior. They were also more likely to mention rules and describe desirable behavior as part of their feedback.
- *Communicating information.* The best classroom managers were better at presenting information, directions, and objectives.

Effective classroom teachers were highly organized, and transitions between activities were conducted efficiently. They maximized student attention and task engagement. Subsequent research has supported this finding at both the elementary and secondary levels.

What We Know

Classroom management works best when the following principles are embedded:

- Emphasize student expectations for behavior.
- Support the learning environment by promoting active learning and student involvement.
- Identify the behaviors that are an integral part of the instructional agenda.
- Have a support system in place so that problem behaviors can be addressed.

Authors' Note

This chapter is an edited version of the American Psychological Association's Teachers' Module on Classroom Management (see www.apa.org/education/k12/classroom-mgmt.aspx).

About the Authors

Thomas Kratochwill is the Sears-Bascom Professor at the University of Wisconsin–Madison. He is the director of the School Psychology Program and a researcher in the Wisconsin Center for Education Research. His research interests focus on evidence-based practices and interventions for children.

Rachel DeRoos is a graduate student in the School Psychology Program at the University of Wisconsin–Madison. Her research interests include mastery-oriented curriculum and family interventions.

Samantha Blair is a graduate student in the School Psychology Program at the University of Wisconsin–Madison. Her research interests include early intervention, socioemotional health, and home-school partnerships.

References and Further Reading

Crone, D. H., Horner, R. H., & Hawken, L. S. (2010). *Responding to behavior problems in schools: The behavior education program* (2nd ed.). New York: Guilford.

Emmer, E., Evertson, C., & Anderson, L. (1980). Effective classroom management at the beginning of the school year. *Elementary School Journal, 80,* 219–231.

Emmer, E. T., & Sabornie, E. J. (Eds.). (2015). *Handbook of classroom management* (2nd ed.). New York: Taylor & Francis.

Evertson, C., & Emmer, E. (1982). Effective management at the beginning of the school year in junior high classes. *Journal of Educational Psychology, 74,* 485–498.

Evertson, C., & Weinstein, C. (Eds.). (2006). *Handbook of classroom management: Research, practice, and contemporary issues.* Mahwah, NJ: Lawrence Erlbaum.

Good Instruction Is Good Classroom Management

Robert Slavin

Robert Slavin explains how exciting, engaging lessons can solve most problems in the classroom.

With the sound of the school bell still echoing in the hall, Julia Carter started her high school English class.

"Today," she began, "you will become thieves. Worse than thieves. Thieves steal only your money or your property. You"—she looked around the class and paused for emphasis—"will steal something far more valuable. You will steal an author's style."

During her speech, the students sat in rapt attention. Two children, Mark and Gloria, slunk in late. Mark made a funny "oops, I'm late" face and did an exaggerated tiptoe to his desk. Ms. Carter ignored both of them, as did the class. She continued her lesson.

While Ms. Carter talked, Mark made an exaggerated show of getting out his books. He whispered to a neighboring student. Without stopping her lesson, Ms. Carter moved near Mark. He stopped whispering and paid attention.

"Today you will become Hemingway. You will steal his words, his pace, his meter, his similes, his metaphors, and will put them to work in your own stories."

Ms. Carter had students review elements of Hemingway's style, which the class had studied before.

"In a moment," she said, "you're going to get your chance to become Ernest Hemingway. As usual, you'll be working in your writing response groups. Before we start, however, let's go over our rules about effective group work. Who can tell me what they are?"

The students volunteered several rules: Respect others, explain your ideas, be sure everyone participates, stand up for your opinion, keep voices low.

"All right," said Ms. Carter. "When I say begin, I'd like you to move your desks together and start planning your compositions. Ready? Begin."

The students moved their desks together smoothly and quickly and got to work. During the transition, Ms. Carter called Mark and Gloria to her desk to discuss their lateness. Gloria had a good excuse, but Mark was developing a pattern of lateness and disruptiveness. Ms. Carter asked Mark to come after school to make a plan to improve his behavior. He then returned to his group and got to work. The students worked in a controlled but excited way through the end of the lesson, thoroughly enjoying "stealing" from Hemingway. The classroom sounded like a beehive with busy, involved students sharing ideas, reading drafts to each other, and editing each other's compositions.

Creating an Effective Learning Environment

The most effective approach to classroom management is effective instruction. Students who are participating in well-structured activities that engage their interests, who are highly motivated to learn, and who are working on tasks that are challenging yet within their capabilities rarely pose any serious management problems. The vignette involving Ms. Carter illustrates this. She has a well-managed class—not because she behaves like a drill sergeant but because she teaches interesting lessons, engages students' imaginations and energies, makes efficient use of time, and communicates a sense of purpose, high expectations, and contagious enthusiasm. However, even a well-managed class is sure to contain individual students who will misbehave. While Ms. Carter's focus is on preventing behavior problems, she is also ready to intervene when necessary to see that students' behaviors are within acceptable limits. For some students, a glance, physical proximity, or a hand on the shoulder is enough. For others, consequences might be necessary. Even in these cases, Ms. Carter does not let behavior issues disrupt her lesson or her students' learning activities.

There is no magic or charisma that makes a teacher an effective classroom manager. Setting up an effective learning environment is a matter of knowing a set of techniques that any teacher can learn and apply.

Effective Use of Time

The first focus of classroom management must be on how time for instruction and learning can be maximized.

1. Preventing Lost Time

Making good use of all classroom time is less a matter of squeezing out a few more minutes or hours of teaching each year than of communicating to students that learning is an important business worthy of their time and effort. If a teacher finds excuses not to teach, students might think that learning is not a serious enterprise.

In studying an outstanding inner-city Baltimore elementary school, a journalist described a third-grade teacher who took her class to the school library, which she found locked. She sent a student for the key, and while the class waited, the teacher whispered to her students, "Let's work on our doubles. Nine plus nine? Six plus six?" The class whispered the answers back in unison. Did a couple of minutes working on addition facts increase the students' achievement? Of course not. But it probably did help to develop a perception that school is for learning, not for marking time.

2. Preventing Late Starts

A surprising amount of instructional time is lost because the teacher does not start teaching at the beginning of the period. A crisp, on-time start to a lesson is important for setting a purposive tone to instruction. If students know that a teacher does not start promptly, they might be lackadaisical about getting to class on time. This attitude makes future on-time starts increasingly difficult. In Ms. Carter's class, students know that if they are late, they will miss something interesting, fun, and important. As a result, almost all of them are in class and ready to learn when the lesson starts.

3. Preventing Interruptions

One important cause of lost allocated time for instruction is interruptions. Interruptions may be externally imposed, such as announcements or the need to sign forms sent from the principal's office, or they may be caused by teachers or students themselves. Interruptions not only cut directly into instruction time but also break the momentum of the lesson, which reduces students' attention to the task at hand.

Avoiding interruptions takes planning. For example, some teachers keep a box where students and others can put any forms, and then they deal with them while students are doing independent or group work or after the lesson is over. Anything that can be postponed until after a lesson should be postponed.

4. Handling Routine Procedures

Teachers should develop routines for simple classroom tasks. For example, many teachers establish a routine that students are only called to line up for lunch when the entire table (or row) is quiet and ready to go. It then takes seconds, not minutes. Exactly how tasks are done is less important than students knowing clearly what they are to do. Many teachers assign regular classroom helpers to take care of distribution and collection of papers, taking messages to the office, and other routine tasks that are annoying interruptions for teachers but that students love to do. Use student power as much as possible.

5. Getting Students' Attention

Teachers need a method for getting students' attention quickly. Many use a "zero noise signal" in which they raise their hand and teach students to raise their own hands, stop talking, and listen. They then praise the groups that comply first. Other teachers use a bell or a tambourine for the same purpose.

6. Maintaining a Rapid Pace of Instruction

Teachers who cover a lot of content in each lesson have students who learn more. A rapid pace also contributes to students' interest and time on task.

7. Minimizing Time Spent on Discipline

Whenever possible, disciplinary statements or actions should not interrupt the flow of the lesson. A sharp glance, silently moving close to an offending student, or a hand signal, such as putting finger to lips to remind a student to be silent, is usually effective for the kind of minor behavior problems that teachers must constantly deal with, and they allow the lesson to proceed without interruption.

Effective classroom management is just informed common sense. Exciting, engaging lessons with real "pizzazz" solve most problems, and simple strategies for effective use of time, like those discussed in this chapter, add to a sense of purpose and prevent most disciplinary problems. Teachers still need to be ready to deal with more serious problems, but in a well-managed, well-taught class, these should be rare. Happy, productive, successful kids are generally well behaved, and well-managed classes let teachers focus on content rather than discipline.

What We Know

- The most effective approach to classroom management is effective teaching.
- Well-managed classes let teachers focus on content.
- There are a number of techniques that can be used by teachers to create an effective learning environment.
- Students who are excited and engaged in challenging tasks rarely pose management problems.

Author's Note

Portions of this chapter are adapted from the 10th edition of *Educational Psychology: Theory and Practice* (Slavin, 2012). Reprinted by permission of Pearson Education, Inc., Upper Saddle River, NJ.

About the Author

Robert Slavin is the director of the Center for Research and Reform in Education at Johns Hopkins School of Education, a professor in the Institute for Effective Education at the University of York, and the driving force behind the Success for All Foundation, a nonprofit organization dedicated to the development, evaluation, and dissemination of research-proven reform models for preschool, elementary, middle, and high schools, especially those serving many children considered at risk.

References and Further Reading

Charles, C. M. (2008). *Building classroom discipline* (9th ed.). Boston: Allyn & Bacon.

Emmer, E. T., & Evertson, C. M. (Eds.). (2009). *Classroom management for middle and high school teachers*. Upper Saddle River, NJ: Pearson.

Jones, V., & Jones, L. (Eds.). (2010). *Comprehensive classroom management* (9th ed.). Upper Saddle River, NJ: Merrill.

Slavin, R. E. (2012). *Educational psychology: Theory and practice* (10th ed.). Boston: Pearson.

Am I the Only One Struggling With Classroom Management?

Inge Poole and Carolyn Evertson

> **Inge Poole** and **Carolyn Evertson** discuss how collaborating professionally with peers, reading relevant research, and participating in classroom management training are valuable tools for meeting challenges in the classroom.

Consistently across the past forty years, teachers list classroom management as a critical concern. However, the individual classroom teacher often feels he or she is the only one experiencing this. In fact, many teachers struggle silently with difficulties for fear of being seen as a potential failure by peers. New teachers, especially, can fear the repercussions of sharing their sense of inadequacy with experienced colleagues or administrators.

To compound this difficulty, the hallmark of great classroom management is an invisible, seamless system. So even if a teacher struggling with classroom management watches a peer's classroom management in action, the details sought may be inaccessible. Three worthwhile tools are available to teachers: collaborating professionally with peers, reading and applying relevant research, and participating in classroom management training.

Collaborating Professionally With Peers

When teachers collaborate professionally with peers, they can do so informally (e.g., between classes) or formally (e.g., at meetings). While the collaboration may have been prompted by the days' events or individuals' feelings, the purpose of the gathering is more than cathartic. Professional collaboration focuses on specific teaching questions that individuals want to pursue together. The individuals or group may do the following:

- Listen carefully for underlying classroom issues.
- Bring to light any actions taken to evaluate their effectiveness.
- Offer suggestions for the future.
- Highlight any training or research to consider.
- Encourage and empower the individuals or group toward effective action.

Professional collaboration is particularly important with classroom management because of its direct impact on instruction. When issues arise with orchestrating the physical, social-emotional, and academic spaces of the classroom, a teacher's peers may have worked previously with similar equipment, students, and/or content. They may have relationships with students' families or connections with resource personnel that open new options to the struggling teacher.

Reading and Applying Relevant Research

Classroom management is a field that has not always had a centralized source of research information. Therefore, reading and applying relevant research in classroom management may require searching in the teacher's field of study (e.g., early education, foreign language), in the area of difficulty (e.g., student defiance, callouts), or in specialized publications on classroom management (e.g., the *Handbook of Classroom Management* [Evertson & Weinstein, 2006]) or instruction (e.g., *21st Century Education: A Reference Handbook* [Good, 2008]).

When a teacher locates research to assist with his or her specific situation(s), it is helpful to note the level of resonance that the research situation has with the teacher's. For example, if an elementary school teacher is reading classroom management research on lab techniques in a high school chemistry class, the transfer of the findings will likely be limited. However, if the elementary school teacher reads through a study on the resolution of playground issues for a group of kindergartners, the research findings may resonate well.

Some key research findings in the field of classroom management include the following:

- Teachers' proactive planning allows the classroom environment to be structured, safe, and supportive of learning.
- Teachers' consistency and clarity in teaching and in reinforcing their expectations enable students to engage with content and behave in ways that allow others to engage as well.
- Teachers who have outstanding classroom management, according to parents, administrators, students, and peers, are seen as "warm demanders" (combining care for students with a demand for mutual respect and high expectations of student effort).

Participating in Classroom Management Training

A third tool for teachers to enhance their classroom management is participation in classroom management training. In-service training provides the opportunity for teachers to consider situations from a new perspective, learn about techniques that have success, and/or evaluate their own classroom management practices. Programs that are research-based and research-proven are especially effective at increasing the participating teachers' skill in classroom management.

The Classroom Organization and Management Program (COMP) of Vanderbilt University is one such research-based, research-proven program. Established on the research agenda of what makes effective classroom managers, COMP shares with participants both seminal and recent research on classroom management, as well as feedback and contributions from thousands of classroom teachers. The program is designed for both the elementary and secondary levels. COMP's theme is to make visible the invisible expectations of teaching.

Four premises frame the program's content: proactive planning, quality instruction, active student engagement, and professional collaboration. Teachers are more effective when they are proactive in their planning for all aspects of classroom life. For example, classrooms that are arranged with forethought to traffic patterns, access points, safety needs, and teaching goals yield increased connections of learners with content. Similarly, classroom procedures that are prudently planned in advance help students meet teachers' expectations, enhancing the social-emotional safety of the classroom.

Effective classroom management is integrally connected with quality classroom teaching. An adage echoing this states, "A good management plan is a great lesson plan." When teachers convey content through a variety of well-planned activities intended to reach the diversity of their classes, they provide the structure of the teaching along with the key concepts of their subject. This enables students to stay engaged, follow directions, identify critical components, participate in formative assessments, ask questions, and demonstrate their understanding of the lessons taught.

The COMP workshop is designed to serve as a model-in-brief of a classroom. This includes the role of active engagement in learning. Workshop leaders engage teachers with the content in ways that are resonant with the research and techniques presented. Participants in COMP share their teaching concerns, successes, and questions with peers as they explore several key areas of classroom management:

- Physical arrangement of the classroom
- Social structure of the classroom
- Student work and accountability
- Consequences and intervention strategies
- Instructional planning
- Student engagement
- Start of school
- Classroom climate and communication
- Student self-monitoring

With each area, participants analyze examples of actual classrooms (e.g., vignettes, charts, data) in relation to the research presented. They then consider how to apply these same principles in their own classrooms, sharing successful strategies in small groups and requesting suggestions on self-identified needs. Teachers set goals in each area covered and revisit their attempts, successes, and continuing needs at a follow-up session.

Key to the effectiveness of COMP is the intentionality of professional collaboration. The workshop is designed to develop a professional learning community in which teachers feel safe to explore the content, identify areas of need in their classrooms, and share professionally with peers. When teachers complete the program, they report a number of successes, including enhanced teacher effectiveness, increased job satisfaction, and decreased office referrals for misbehaving students. Students of these teachers demonstrate increased academic achievement and improved behavior. These results hold true for both regular and special education classes across the K–12 spectrum.

Conclusion

Teachers may feel they are alone in experiencing difficulties with classroom management. Fortunately, there are tools that can help them to connect with others who experience similar challenges and learn ways to enhance their classroom management skills. Professional collaboration with peers enables teachers to feel part of the profession and benefit from the experience and expertise of others. Reading and applying relevant research helps teachers see the commonalities of the teaching experience and adopt best practices in their teaching. Participating in classroom management training enables teachers to learn more about and enhance their skill in classroom management. When the selected in-service training is research-based and research-proven and includes professional collaboration, as with COMP, teachers can see results such as increased skill, improved job satisfaction, decreased misbehavior and office referrals, and increased student achievement.

What We Know

- *All* teachers experience classroom management challenges; therefore, teachers' professional collaboration builds community, provides support, and improves teaching (including classroom management).
- Research on classroom management identifies specific approaches, techniques, and attitudes that teachers can use with success.
- Teachers who participate in classroom management training can enhance their skill in classroom management. This in turn can increase their job satisfaction as well as students' on-task behavior and academic achievement.
- Effective classroom management is most frequently seen in the classrooms of "warm demanders"—teachers who demonstrate care for students and simultaneously hold students to high academic and behavioral expectations.

About the Authors

Inge Poole is a lead national trainer with the COMP Program at Vanderbilt University. Her research interests include classroom management and teacher identity.

Carolyn Evertson is a professor emerita at Peabody College, Vanderbilt University. Her research on classroom management includes numerous publications, the development of COMP as a program for teachers, and coeditorship of the *Handbook of Research on Classroom Management* with Carol Weinstein, who is a professor emerita at Rutgers University.

References and Further Reading

Classroom Organization and Management Program. Retrieved from www.comp.org

Evertson, C., & Poole, I. (2008). Proactive classroom management. In T. Good (Ed.), *21st century education: A reference handbook* (Vol. 1, pp. 131–139). Thousand Oaks, CA: Sage.

Evertson, C., & Weinstein, C. (Eds.). (2006). *Handbook of classroom management: Research, practice, and contemporary issues.* Mahwah, NJ: Lawrence Erlbaum.

Good, T. (Ed.). (2008). *21st century education: A reference handbook* (Vol. 1). Thousand Oaks, CA: Sage.

Poole, I., & Evertson, C. (2013). Elementary classroom management. In J. Hattie & E. Anderman (Eds.), *International guide to student achievement* (pp. 188–191). New York: Routledge.

16

Classroom Management

What Teachers Should Know

Regina Oliver

Regina Oliver *provides some practical advice for teachers, culled from a systematic review of the research on classroom management.*

Teachers who struggle with classroom management experience a high level of stress and burnout. "I love teaching and would do it forever if it wasn't for the difficult student behavior in my classroom." "I've tried everything but nothing seems to help." These are common sentiments held by many teachers. Teachers enter the profession because of their desire to teach but often find themselves ill-prepared to manage the challenges of classroom behavior management. More and more students are entering school without the behavioral competencies needed to meet the instructional and social demands of the classroom environment. Teachers frequently report a lack of training in their teacher preparation programs to effectively manage an increasingly diverse student population. Without the skills needed to establish structured, positive environments that support student behavior, teachers quickly become overwhelmed, and many ultimately leave the profession.

The negative impact of ineffective classroom management is also evident with regard to student outcomes. Classrooms in which the teacher struggles with managing classroom behavior tend to have higher rates of disruptive student behavior and decreased instructional time. Consequently, students in these classrooms typically perform lower on academic assignments and achievement tests. Students who are already at risk for behavior problems are disproportionately affected by the social context of the classroom environment, as aggressive student behavior is maintained or made worse by ineffective classroom management practices. Teachers play an important role in the social development of their students and the prevention of behavior problems and disorders. Effective classroom management practices are vital not only to teacher persistence in the field but also to achieving social and academic competence for all students.

Classroom Management Research

Although the challenges of managing the classroom and student behavior may seem daunting, researchers have fortunately identified effective strategies for meeting these challenges. Teachers should develop classroom management plans prior to the beginning of the school year that build the foundation for effective behavior support. Researchers recommend the following:

1. *Be proactive to prevent inappropriate student behavior rather than rely on reactive, punitive approaches.* Teachers can be proactive by carefully considering how the classroom will be set up and managed throughout the school day and across the school year, taking into consideration which times of day and year may be more problematic and require increased structure. Prevention also means using strategies like proactive prompts to cue students in to behavioral expectations before an activity begins, thereby preventing problematic behavior.

2. *Explicitly teach students classroom expectations and routines.* Teachers cannot assume students will know how to behave in their classroom. Behavioral expectations (e.g., be prepared, be respectful, be responsible) and classroom routines for such things as turning in homework, moving into cooperative learning groups, or asking the teacher for assistance should all be explicitly taught at the beginning of and throughout the school year.

3. *Provide multiple ways to acknowledge appropriate behavior using behavior-specific praise and other reinforcement strategies (e.g., token economy).* Teaching rules and routines alone will not ensure that students will continue using these skills. Teachers should "catch students being good" and provide multiple ways to acknowledge appropriate behavior. Behavior-specific praise that identifies the particular behavior being praised is a very powerful strategy.

4. *Use a continuum of strategies to respond to inappropriate behavior, including reteaching desired expectations.* Despite the emphasis teachers place on being proactive to prevent inappropriate behavior, it will inevitably occur. Teachers should use multiple strategies, such as proximity control, verbal prompts and redirection, or behavioral contracts, based on the severity of student behavior. If inappropriate behavior occurs, it should be treated as a behavioral error and appropriate behavior retaught.

5. *Monitor student behavior and the effectiveness of the classroom management plan and make adjustments as needed according to the data.* Monitoring

student behavior means that teachers are aware of what students are doing at all times and are able to stop minor disruptive behavior from escalating. If students are frequently asking questions about classroom routines or are being disruptive, the classroom management plan may need to be adjusted or expectations and routines retaught.

A Systematic Review of Classroom Management Research

While recommendations from researchers regarding the use of specific classroom management strategies are useful, a systematic review of the literature provides quantifiable data regarding the outcomes teachers can expect when classroom management approaches are implemented. For the purposes of the review, classroom management is defined as a collection of nonteaching classroom procedures implemented by teachers in classroom settings with all students for the purposes of teaching prosocial behavior and preventing and reducing inappropriate behavior. We conducted a systematic review, called a meta-analysis, to determine which classroom management programs are more or less effective. Database searches and screening procedures of 5,134 titles produced twelve studies that met inclusion criteria.

The analysis across the twelve studies indicates a statistically significant effect of classroom management on reducing aggressive, disruptive student behavior with students in kindergarten through twelfth grade. Students in the treatment classrooms in all twelve studies showed less disruptive, inappropriate, and aggressive behavior in the classroom, compared to students in the control classrooms. These outcomes are even more significant because these effects were found in comparison to classrooms in which teachers were using standard classroom management practices, rather than no classroom management. That is, teachers who use effective classroom management can expect to experience improvements in student behavior over and above typical or less systematic classroom management practices.

Implications for Teachers

The results of the systematic review provide useful information and have important implications for teachers. Evidence-based classroom management approaches exist and are important in establishing and maintaining classroom environments where students spend less time being disruptive and more time engaged in academic tasks. Teachers who develop a classroom management plan that includes necessary features, such as teaching students classroom rules and routines and reinforcing or praising appropriate behavior, will reap the benefits of a smoother running classroom. Once the teacher has an effective classroom-wide behavior management plan in place and there are low levels of disruptive behavior, there is more time to spend on students who may require additional support. Keep in mind that classroom organization and behavior management plans may need to be changed, based on how students are responding.

What We Know

- The progression of behavior issues is influenced by teacher classroom management practices in the early years.
- Several evidence-based classroom management strategies have been identified through research.
- Teachers who use a proactive classroom-behavior-management plan will have fewer disruptive behaviors and will be more successful with students who require more intensive behavioral support.
- Pre-service and in-service teacher preparation is needed to provide teachers with the necessary classroom management competencies to support student behavior.

About the Author

Regina Oliver is an assistant research professor in the Center for Child and Family Well-Being in the Special Education and Communication Disorders Department at the University of Nebraska–Lincoln. Dr. Oliver has published and conducted research in teacher preparation, evaluation of effective classroom organization and behavior management, and the improvement of teacher use of evidence-based classroom management practices. She also has extensive experience working with school systems to implement schoolwide and individualized positive behavioral support and classroom management systems.

Reference and Further Reading

Oliver, R. M., Wehby, J. H., & Reschly, D. (2011, June). Teacher classroom management practices: Effects on disruptive or aggressive student behavior. *Campbell Systematic Reviews*. Retrieved from from http://campbellcollaboration.org

17

From Tourists to Citizens

H. Jerome Freiberg

H. Jerome Freiberg describes Consistency Management & Cooperative Discipline (CMCD), an approach rooted in person-centered psychology.

The educational landscape is in disequilibrium. Society has become more complex, and this complexity is reflected in the microsocieties of schools and classrooms. Historically, young people have been sustained and nurtured by five pillars of support: family, community, culture, religion, and school. Four of these five pillars are in flux in a changing society. Schools, the fifth pillar, are expected to carry an ever-increasing social-emotional and academic load. Schools are also in transformation, becoming more bureaucratic and rule-based. Subsequently, parent-school and community relationships are more formalized, with students and parents becoming educational tourists who are just passing through rather than engaged citizens. Adding to this, technology is shifting the paradigm of how and where information is acquired. The schoolhouse and its educators are no longer the sole source of information, creating social uncertainty. Student behavior and classroom management become a flashpoint of this uncertainty, as current management systems may lack the flexibility to respond to these rapid changes.

This chapter describes a prosocial, person-centered approach to classroom management: CMCD. For the past twenty years, CMCD has proven to be a resourceful evidence-based alternative, going beyond standard behavioral classroom management models of compliance and obedience to help children and young people build the self-discipline they need to excel in an ever-changing world. CMCD emphasizes a multilayered Behavioral, Instructional, and Organizational (BIO) classroom management approach that provides teachers, administrators, students, and school staff with the tools they need to build community and organizational capacity within their classrooms and schools.

Classroom management is more than student discipline. The CMCD model seeks to turn passive tourists into engaged citizens in a classroom where cooperation, participation, and support are the cornerstones. The CMCD program combines instructional effectiveness (through consistency of organization in the classroom) with student self-discipline (developed cooperatively with teachers).

CMCD emphasizes prevention first and intervention second. This provides opportunities for student self-discipline through student engagement, a positive school and classroom climate, and instructional time management, resulting in greater student learning. CMCD can be implemented in individual teachers' classrooms or schoolwide. Furthermore, CMCD is not limited to a single age group; the program has been effectively implemented at all levels, from Head Start through high school.

So how exactly does it work? Rooted in person-centered psychology, CMCD presents a system for creating a balance between the needs of the teacher and learner. To facilitate BIO management, five key themes—prevention, caring, cooperation, organization, and community—allow teachers and students to share classroom responsibilities and build meaningful relationships.

Five Consistency Management & Cooperative Discipline Themes

Prevention

Teachers are encouraged to prevent problems before they begin by providing students with a consistent, flexible, and active learning environment.

Caring

Students want to know how much you care before they want to learn how much you know. Students learn how to solve disputes, prevent problems, and work and learn in groups all within a supportive, caring environment. The teacher's role is to create fair, consistent, and engaging instruction with predictable daily classroom routines. The goal of consistency management is to enable students to feel comfortable, cared for, and at liberty to take intellectual risks in a predictable, flexible learning environment. Classrooms become the key environment for change, as teachers facilitate the transit of students from tourists to citizens.

Cooperation

Teachers are encouraged to provide students with opportunities for cooperative discipline, starting with the rules in the form of a classroom constitution. All students are given the opportunity to become leaders in the classroom with "job" responsibilities as CMCD one-minute managers. Students apply and interview for classroom positions, including substitute teacher manager and student absence manager.

Organization

Assignments, objectives for the lesson, and homework are listed daily on the board or on the teacher's blog. Questions are asked randomly using a "Go-Around Cup." A countdown poster near the door or a digital reminder charts project due dates and timelines. Overall, the teacher's role within CMCD is to fashion a support system with learners in which students are active citizens, not passive tourists.

Community

Each person has a voice in the operations of the classroom. During classroom meetings, student opinions and perspectives are heard. Students need to see people in the school and classroom who are not paid to be there. Community organizations and leaders are invited into the classroom. Parents attend workshops for CMCD at home, and teachers are provided with a range of parent connectedness activities such as "Bring a Smile Note Home" or a "Vine of Kindness for the Home."

The five themes provide educators with a predictable and engaging classroom. Table 17.1 outlines teacher-centered and CMCD-centered classrooms.

Table 17.1   Teacher-Centered and Person-Centered Orientations to Classroom Management

Teacher-Centered Classrooms	CMCD Person-Centered Classrooms
Teacher is the sole leader	Leadership is shared
Management is a form of oversight	Management is a form of guidance
Teacher takes responsibility for all the paperwork and organization	Students are facilitators for the functions of the classroom
Discipline comes from the teacher	Discipline comes from the self
A few students are the teacher's helpers	All students have the opportunity to become an integral part of the management of the classroom
Teacher makes the rules and posts them for the students	Rules are developed by the teacher and students in the form of a classroom constitution or compact
Consequences are fixed for all students	Consequences reflect individual differences
Rewards are mostly extrinsic	Rewards are mostly intrinsic
Students are allowed limited responsibilities	Students share in classroom manager responsibilities
Few members of the community enter the classroom	Partnerships are formed with business and community groups to enrich and broaden the learning opportunities for students

Source: Freiberg (1999). © H. Jerome Freiberg. Used with permission.

Research Support

The CMCD program has been researched in studies over time. The findings from both qualitative and quantitative studies show a strong positive change in many of the outcomes viewed as desirable for reforming schools and transforming class-rooms. Research on past person-centered and student-centered learning studies found positive cognitive and emotional learner outcomes in person-centered environments, including creativity and critical thinking, self-esteem, and a reduction in dropouts.

The following CMCD findings are found in the research literature:

- Significant increase in teacher and student attendance
- A 45 to 78 percent reduction in office discipline referrals
- Significant increase in student achievement in math and reading, with effect-size gains that equate to one-third to three-fourths of a year's gain in math and reading on state and national tests
- Improvement in classroom and school climate
- External researchers report CMCD teachers having from 2.5 to 5.4 weeks more time to teach—time previously used for discipline or management purposes
- Significant improvement of students' sense of ownership in urban elementary schools
- Students use more comprehensive strategies for learning when compared with non-CMCD schools

A Climate for Learning

Although we teach about democracy, rarely do we practice it in our schools. CMCD bridges this gap by creating caring classrooms and supportive schools that provide students the opportunity to become a citizen through experiential learning. In places where people respect each other, learn from mistakes, and build upon successes, students can become informed and involved members of a democratic society.

What We Know

- A review of 800 discipline/management programs by fourteen external organizations found few had research to support their program outcomes.
- Time gained or lost to behavior directly affects student achievement.
- Meta-analyses conclude the following:
  - Elementary school mathematics achievement is enhanced by classroom management that affects daily classroom practices.
  - Person-centered classroom management improves both socioemotional and cognitive development.
  - Classroom management is the first of the top five factors influencing school learning.

About the Author

H. Jerome Freiberg is a John and Rebecca Moores Professor in the College of Education, University of Houston, and has over 100 scholarly publications. He is a fellow of the American Educational Research Association (AERA), founder of CMCD, editor of the *Journal of Classroom Interaction,* received the 2013 AERA Classroom Management Special Interest Group (SIG) Carol Weinstein Best Paper Award, and has taught in middle school, high school, and a maximum security prison.

References and Further Reading

Freiberg, H. J. (Ed.). (1999). *Beyond behaviorism: Changing the classroom management paradigm.* Boston: Allyn & Bacon.

Freiberg, H. J. (2013). Classroom management and student achievement. In J. Hattie & E. Anderman (Eds.), *International guide to student achievement* (pp. 228–230). New York: Routledge.

Freiberg, H. J., & Driscoll, A. (2005). *Universal teaching strategies* (4th ed.). Boston: Allyn & Bacon.

Freiberg, H. J., Huzinec, C. A., & Templeton, S. M. (2009). Classroom management—A pathway to student achievement: A study of fourteen inner-city elementary schools. *Elementary School Journal, 110*(1), 63–80.

Freiberg, H. J., & Lamb, S. M. (2009). Dimensions of person-centered classroom management. *Theory into Practice, 48,* 99–105.

Freiberg, H. J., Templeton, S., & Helton, S. (2013). Classroom management: A pathway to improving school climate in two British secondary schools. In M. Newberry, A. Gallant, & P. Riley (Eds.), *Emotion in school: Understanding how the hidden curriculum influences relationships, leadership, teaching and learning* (pp. 203–225). Bingley, UK: Emerald.

Promoting Engagement With Check & Connect

Angie Pohl and Karen Storm

Angie Pohl and **Karen Storm** show how student engagement can be supported with the Check & Connect program.

The first advice new teachers receive about managing a classroom is to ensure that all students are fully engaged in learning. When children are meaningfully engaged in their learning, they are less likely to display disruptive behaviors, and teachers are able to focus on teaching rather than on discipline. Although engagement can be achieved for all learners, not all are engaged through universal school practices and core instruction. According to the Response to Intervention (RTI) model of tiered instructional support, educators can expect approximately 80 percent of their students to respond to universal interventions and engage in their learning, while 15 to 20 percent require supplemental intervention to do so. Check & Connect is a supplemental student engagement intervention intended to complement universal-level practices. Check & Connect serves marginalized, disengaged students and promotes their engagement at school and with learning.

In Check & Connect, student engagement is defined as the student's active participation in academic and cocurricular or school-related activities and as commitment to educational goals and learning. Student engagement is a multidimensional construct, which includes academic, behavioral, cognitive, and affective subtypes:

- Academic and behavioral engagement involve observable indicators from data readily available in schools.
  - *Academic engagement* is observed through such indicators as the amount of time spent doing schoolwork or related projects in school or at home, time on task, number of credits accrued, amount of homework completed with accuracy, and course grades—especially the number of failing grades.

○ *Behavioral engagement* is reflected in such indicators as attendance, effort and active participation in class, involvement in extracurricular activities, and behavioral incidents such as detentions and suspensions.

- Cognitive and affective engagement represent internal indicators that are less observable and require an understanding of the student perspective:
  ○ *Cognitive engagement* is expressed in self-regulated learning strategies, goal setting, interest in learning, motivation to learn, and student perception of the relevance of school to personal aspirations, the value of learning, and control of and competence in schoolwork.
  ○ *Affective engagement* refers to a sense of belonging and connection to school and availability of quality support from parents, teachers, and peers.

The subtypes of engagement are interrelated. For example, a student's feelings of belonging (affective engagement) may promote greater effort and participation on the student's part (behavioral engagement); teaching practices that promote strategy use or self-regulation (cognitive engagement) may also facilitate greater time on task or homework completion with high success rates (academic engagement).

How Does Check & Connect Promote Student Engagement?

Check & Connect promotes engagement through a structured mentoring intervention with a clear set of procedures and elements.

Procedures

The mentor regularly "checks" on students' educational progress using data on alterable variables collected by schools such as grades, credits earned, behavior referrals, and attendance. The mentor then uses the data gathered to "connect" with students and implement timely, individualized interventions to reestablish and maintain the student's connection to school and learning. The mentor also connects and engages with families to strengthen the family-school relationship. Mentors recognize the importance of multiple contextual influences—home, school, and community—for fostering student learning and work to create positive relationships in and among all three environments.

Core Elements

1. *Relationships.* Mentors make a long-term commitment to students and build relationships with them based on mutual trust and open communication. The focus on alterable variables, personalized intervention, commitment, and participation are essential, readily operationalized elements for building relationships with students.

2. *Problem solving and capacity building.* Cognitive problem solving is taught to and used with students to empower them to identify and address barriers to their school success. Mentors promote the acquisition of problem-solving skills to resolve conflicts constructively, encourage the search for solutions rather than a source of blame, foster productive coping skills, and diminish dependency on the mentor.

3. *Persistence-plus.* Persistence-plus refers to persistence, continuity, and consistency. Persistence means there is someone who believes in students' ability to learn and does not allow young people to be distracted from the importance of school and learning. Continuity means there is someone who knows students' educational history, is familiar with their family background, and is available throughout the school year, the summer, and into the next year. Consistency means mentors reinforce the same message—a caring adult believes school and learning are important and that students can learn and succeed in school.

What Is the Evidence Base for Check & Connect?

Research on Check & Connect began in 1990. Rigorous research has shown that Check & Connect significantly increases the likelihood that students will stay in school. Check & Connect is the only dropout prevention intervention reviewed by the U.S. Department of Education's What Works Clearinghouse to show "positive effects" for staying in school, based on data gathered through two randomized controlled trials (RCTs) with high school students with disabilities, and four replication studies with K–12 students with and without disabilities. Other findings from Check & Connect research studies indicate that Check & Connect has been shown to improve the following:

- Enrollment, attendance, and odds of graduation for students who are disengaged or at risk of dropping out of school
- Engagement and attendance for elementary students
- School outcomes for students with a history of truancy

Lessons Learned

Over the past twenty-four years, we have learned many lessons about implementing Check & Connect and promoting student engagement—lessons that are applicable at both the individual student level and the classroom level.

First, we have learned about the power, value, and importance of personalized interventions—interventions that create a person-environment fit—for engaging students who are disengaged or at risk of dropout. Although Check & Connect is a structured intervention, it is not prescriptive. Interventions align with student needs and alterable indicators of risk (e.g., grades, credits, behavior) and utilize available resources. Promoting a person-environment fit may require changes to the learning environment. Mentors, however, do not assume they can alter universal school policies and practices. Instead, they problem-solve with appropriate school personnel to modify the environment to enhance students' sense of belonging, connection at school, and engagement with learning.

Second, relationships are essential for students' behavior change, commitment to learning, and academic progress in school. Check & Connect is a *relationship-based intervention*.

Finally, we have learned the necessity of engaging students academically, behaviorally, cognitively, and affectively. Interventions that seek to fully engage students must attend to the student's beliefs of "I can" (perceptions of competence and control), "I want to" (personal values and goals), and "I belong" (social connectedness to peers and teachers). This expanded framework suggests that understanding students' emotional and intellectual feelings about school is essential for understanding their schooling experiences and academic outcomes. As we implemented Check & Connect, we noted that engagement for students at high risk of educational failure is much more than time on task (i.e., academic engagement) or attendance and participation (i.e., behavioral engagement). Successful implementation of Check & Connect fosters students' perceived connection with others (i.e., affective engagement) and promotes both motivation to learn and perceived relevance of schoolwork for future goals (i.e., cognitive engagement).

What We Know

- Check & Connect, an evidence-based intervention, promotes student engagement.
- Essential Check & Connect components include the following:
  - A mentor who works with students and families for at least two years
  - Regular checks using data on students' educational progress
  - Timely, personalized, data-driven interventions to establish and maintain the student's connection to school and learning
  - Engagement with families

About the Authors

Angie Pohl, PhD, is a research associate at the Institute on Community Integration at the University of Minnesota, conducting research and training for Check & Connect. She was formerly a high school teacher. Her research interests include student engagement, self-regulated learning, and bridging K–12 to college.

Karen Storm, PhD, is a research associate for the Center for Early Education and Development at the University of Minnesota. Her research interests include evaluation studies, improving K–16 retention and engagement, and leadership to support engaging school environments.

References and Further Reading

Appleton, J. J., Christenson, S. L., & Furlong, M. J. (2008). Student engagement with school: Critical conceptual and methodological issues of the construct. *Psychology in the Schools, 45*(5), 369–386.

Check & Connect on What Works Clearinghouse. (2006). Retrieved from http://ies .ed.gov/ncee/wwc/interventionreport.aspx?sid=78

Christenson, S. L., Stout, K., & Pohl, A. (2012). *Check & Connect: A comprehensive student engagement intervention: Implementing with fidelity*. Minneapolis: University of Minnesota, Institute on Community Integration.

National Research Council and the Institute of Medicine. (2004). *Engaging schools: Fostering high school students' motivation to learn*. Washington, DC: The National Academies Press.

Dealing With Classroom Management Problems

Saul Axelrod

Saul Axelrod *explains how applied behavior analysis (ABA) and positive reinforcement can help teachers successfully manage their classrooms.*

There is probably no issue more pressing for teachers than dealing with classroom management problems. Teachers wake up obsessing over a student's behavior or even leave education. Here is what is so sad about this. It is unnecessary. For approximately fifty years, there have been available to teachers ABA interventions that can solve most classroom management problems in a quick and humane manner.

ABA is derived from the basic principles of behavior outlined by famed psychologist B. F. Skinner about three quarters of a century ago. Thousands of journal articles and books have demonstrated that ABA can be used to solve some of the most difficult behavioral problems. Yet, for reasons I have discussed in other articles, ABA is regularly used in special education but seldom used in regular education. This is unfortunate. If ABA procedures were used more often in regular education, inclusion of children with disabilities would be more of a reality in regular education, and teachers' lives would be much happier.

Positive Reinforcement Procedures

There are many complex principles in ABA. Yet by knowing how to apply a relatively simple principle—positive reinforcement—teachers are able to produce large and desirable changes in the behaviors of their students.

The principle of positive reinforcement indicates that when a pleasant event follows a behavior, the behavior is more likely to occur in the future. For example, when teachers compliment students for behaving properly, it is likely that they will behave more appropriately in the future. If the teacher awards extra marks to students for handing homework in on time, the chances are that students will be more diligent in handing in their homework next time.

It is surprising to me that people have so many reservations and concerns about positive reinforcement procedures. The principle of positive reinforcement is a natural, not a contrived, process. People say hello to people who smile back at them. Salespeople make efforts to sell more products because such activities increase their commissions. Athletes try hard to meet the incentive clauses of their contracts.

What Is So Wonderful About Positive Reinforcement Procedures?

There are few things in life that produce only pleasant outcomes. Positive reinforcement comes as close to this ideal as any other process does. Positive reinforcement works quickly and well to change important behaviors and is humane as well. Children love being in a classroom where positive reinforcement procedures are being used. Teachers enjoy teaching with positive reinforcement procedures because the results are so gratifying. Positive reinforcement procedures create a loving bond between students and teachers.

How Do I Find Out What Children's Positive Reinforcers Are?

This is not hard to do. There are a number of actions you can do to find out what a student's *possible* positive reinforcers are. I italicized *possible* because you cannot be sure if an item or activity is a positive reinforcer until you try it out. Here are some things you can do. First, you can ask the child what he or she would like to work for. You can ask the same question to the child's parents. You can also ask them to pick from a list of possible reinforcers. Another way of identifying possible positive reinforcers is to note what a child spends a lot of time doing. If a student frequently runs to the computer, computer time is likely to be a positive reinforcer. Finally, you can observe what follows an inappropriate behavior. This may be a positive reinforcer. For example, if you notice that often when a student storms out of the classroom, he or she gets to spend time with a favorite principal, visiting the principal may be a positive reinforcer. You may then have the child earn time with the principal for behaving *appropriately*.

What Are Some Positive Reinforcers I Can Use?

This is easy. The first one falls under the category of social reinforcement and consists of smiles, compliments, or a call home to a parent reporting how well their child behaved that day. It is helpful to compliment children when they walk into class each day. This prompts appropriate student behavior, which should also be praised. The best predictor I know of for successful classroom management is the number of compliments a teacher gives. The more, the better. Think of how you feel when someone gives you a sincere compliment. Some teachers are admonished not to smile until Christmas. I say, start smiling on Labor Day and keep smiling until Flag Day.

There are also a number of activity and tangible reinforcers for students of all ages. These include having extra free time, collecting student papers, having lunch with the teacher, earning extra points toward a grade, and reading favored materials.

What Are a Few Examples of Successful Applied Behavior Analysis Programs?

Here are a few examples. One first-grade teacher I know had a student who made animal sounds forty-five times per day. The teacher divided the day into fifteen-minute blocks. For every fifteen-minute block without an animal sound, the girl earned a minute on the computer to be enjoyed at the end of the day. The girl then made animal sounds only four times a day.

A middle school teacher found that students were frequently out of their seats. She set a timer to ring three times a lesson at unpredictable intervals. If all students were seated when the timer went off, the group earned a point. Ten points meant a day without homework. Out-of-seat behavior became a rarity.

A high school mathematics teacher found that students were taking a long time to transition between classes. He solved this by putting bonus problems on the whiteboard at the start of each class. The problems were removed after five minutes. Most students arrived at class punctually, thereafter, in order to receive the bonus points on their grades.

What Are Some Pointers for Solving Classroom Problems Constructively?

- *Set reasonable goals.* A small improvement in behavior is appropriate at the start. As student behavior improves, you can increase the requirements for positive reinforcers.
- *Make adjustments in your procedures.* As you use a procedure, you may notice better ways to apply the intervention. Make these changes. A small adjustment in an intervention can produce a major change in the outcome.
- *Talk to other teachers.* You have a lot of smart, skillful colleagues. Talk to them. Ask them what they have found helpful when they have encountered problems similar to yours.
- *Read teacher-oriented ABA textbooks.* They are filled with descriptions of interventions that have been successful with situations like the ones you are encountering.
- *Use interventions that are easy to apply and are inexpensive.* The best procedures are simple and powerful, and they exist. A visit to a dollar store is a good start for inexpensive rewards.

- *Prioritize and work with only one or two behaviors at the start.* There may be several behavior problems in your classroom, but it is too difficult to address all of them at once. Focus on one or two problems. When they come under control, you can add other behaviors to your program. A procedure that is effective with one behavior is likely to be effective with other behaviors.
- *Be an optimist.* The situation may be tough, but it is not impossible. Teachers like you have dealt successfully with more difficult problems. When your intervention does not work, it is not your failure. It is just a prompt to try something else. Giving up is the only failure.
- *Organize all aspects of your teaching activities through checklists.* They work in the building trades, they work in the emergency room, they work in piloting planes, and they work in the classroom.

What We Know

- There is a lot of evidence that ABA can be used to solve some of the most difficult behavioral problems.
- ABA interventions, like positive reinforcement, work well and are easy to implement.
- Students enjoy being in a classroom where positive reinforcement procedures are being used, and teachers enjoy teaching with positive reinforcement procedures because the results are so gratifying.

About the Author

Saul Axelrod is professor emeritus of special education and ABA at Temple University. His research and writings have focused on devising and disseminating procedures that increase teacher effectiveness.

References and Further Reading

Alberto, P. A., & Troutman, A. C. (2009). *Applied behavior analysis for teachers* (8th ed.). Upper Saddle River, NJ: Prentice Hall.

Axelrod, S., Moyer, L., & Berry, B. (1990). Why teachers do not use behavior modification procedures. *Journal of Educational and Psychological Consultation, 1,* 309–320.

Cooper, J. O., Heron, T. E., & Heward, W. L. (2007). *Applied behavior analysis* (2nd ed.). Upper Saddle River, NJ: Prentice Hall.

Kazdin, A. E. (2008). *The Kazdin Method for parenting the defiant child.* Boston: Houghton Mifflin Harcourt.

Support for Teachers Around the World

Judy Hutchings

*The Incredible Years (IY) Teacher Classroom Management (TCM)
program has been shown to be effective in many different countries, as
Judy Hutchings explains.*

The IY series is a suite of evidence-based programs for parents, children, and teachers, developed and researched by Carolyn Webster-Stratton over the past thirty years, for the prevention and treatment of conduct disorder and related difficulties. It has demonstrated effectiveness through many high-quality randomized controlled trials (RCTs). Webster-Stratton has ensured effective dissemination through training, resources, supervision, and leader certification.

The TCM program is delivered to groups of teachers one day a month for five or six months. It improves teacher-student relationships and home-school links, increases teacher competencies, and develops children's social and problem-solving skills. Like the programs for parents and children, strategies in TCM that maximize behavior change include a collaborative delivery style, discussion, observation of videotapes of classroom situations, role-play rehearsal, and classroom-based practice between sessions. Feedback is provided and written assignments are reviewed.

The linked IY children's component, Classroom Dinosaur School program, promotes children's social skills, emotional regulation, and problem-solving skills through a therapeutic intervention and/or a classroom curriculum. The curriculum covers learning school rules, labeling feelings, problem solving, anger management, and friendship skills. These programs use puppets as role models, discussion, observing videotapes of children, role-play rehearsal, and homework.

A number of RCTs have included the TCM and Classroom Dinosaur School programs in various combinations with the parenting program. The TCM and Classroom

Dinosaur School programs showed significant improvements in children's problem solving and peer relationships, as well as teacher behavior.

Around the United Kingdom

Wales

The IY suite of parenting programs has received funding from the English government, and for seven years the Welsh government has allocated funds to train group leaders. The various parent programs have been extensively researched and rolled out, primarily in early intervention settings. Adoption of the TCM and Classroom Dinosaur School programs has been slower, although they are well established in Wales, where they started in 2002. Pilot trials achieved good outcomes. The TCM program was well received, and strategies taught were highly rated by teachers. An RCT showed significant improvements in teacher and child behavior using a specially designed classroom observation tool. Two pilot studies of the Therapeutic Dinosaur School program were effective in improving children's behavior, resulting in a large-scale RCT targeting high-risk young children in twenty-two schools in Wales. Results from this trial showed significant benefits in terms of children's problem-solving skills and achievement of teacher-set personal social development goals for the year for intervention children. Welsh government funding supported the TCM and Classroom Dinosaur School programs with training and resources.

Devon

The TCM program is currently being researched in Devon, where forty teachers from sixteen schools attended TCM training and reported satisfaction with the program. This led to the Supporting Teachers And childRen in Schools (STARS) trial to evaluate whether teacher attendance at the TCM course improves children's social-emotional well-being and academic achievement, and teachers' emotional well-being and sense of professional efficacy.

In this trial, eighty primary schools will be recruited over a three-year period, and each school will take part for three academic years. One teacher from reception to Year 4 (the U.K. equivalent of preK to third grade), the children in their classes, and the children's parents will take part from each school. Schools randomized to the intervention will receive the TCM course. Children's social-emotional well-being is recorded by teachers and parents at the beginning and end of each academic year. Academic progress and scores will be validated against detailed literacy and numeracy assessments for some children. Teachers' sense of effectiveness as a teacher and their emotional well-being will be measured.

The trial started in September 2012, with fifteen schools recruited for the pilot year. A further thirty schools started in September 2013, and we are recruiting the final thirty-five for September 2014.

Around Europe

Ireland

The IY Ireland Study involved three RCTs, one of which evaluated the TCM program. This included a qualitative study and a stand-alone cost-effectiveness analysis. The results demonstrated significant improvements in teachers' classroom management strategies six and twelve months later. Also after six months, aspects of children's behavior improved, especially among children who were most "at risk." Teachers found the TCM principles effective and easy to implement, and children responded well. Significant benefits vis-à-vis teacher stress were also reported. The costs of implementing the IY TCM program were very modest when compared to other education-based programs.

Norway

After piloting the TCM program in schools and kindergartens, the Norwegian IY research group started an evaluation of the program in 2009 with matched schools and kindergartens and randomized assignment of seven students from each class in first to third grade. The trial includes fifty schools and fifty kindergartens, with twenty-five intervention and twenty-five control groups in each. Approximately 4,300 students are involved. The kindergarten group is completed, and the school group post-treatment data will be collected during May and June 2014.

Outcome measures include teacher-child relationships; child behavior problems; child behavior measures; teacher-parent cooperation; and classroom behavior, climate, and behavior measures.

Portugal

Following training, in 2009 the TCM handouts were translated into Portuguese and the program delivered to and evaluated with a group of kindergarten teachers in urban and rural areas. Results were compared with comparison schools, and children were found to be showing more social competence and fewer conduct and behavior problems. Additionally, observations by "blind" coders showed that positive classroom practices improved only in the intervention group. Program satisfaction was very high, and this provided the first evidence of the effectiveness of the program in enhancing protective factors and reducing child risk factors, in a community sample, in Portugal. The TCM program is now being evaluated in a broader research project alongside the parenting program to assess whether the teacher intervention adds to the effects of parental intervention. The trial will finish in 2013.

Further Developments

Jamaica

Helen Baker-Henningham introduced the TCM program into Jamaica and conducted a pilot study in which the TCM program was delivered in combination with sessions from the Dinosaur School curriculum. Teachers' positive behavior and children's appropriate behavior significantly increased following TCM training. She subsequently conducted a cluster RCT of an enhanced version of the program, which included supplementary videotaped material from Jamaican classrooms in twenty-four Jamaican preschools. She reported significant benefits to children's behavior based on observations and on reports from teachers and parents. This work is being further rolled out across Jamaica.

New Zealand

In New Zealand, the IY parenting and TCM programs were included in a larger national initiative managed by the Ministry of Education—the Positive Behavior for Learning (PB4L) Action Plan. Initial outcome measures showed teacher satisfaction and self-reported positive behavior change. Ongoing measures will include the Teacher Strategies and Teacher Satisfaction Questionnaires.

The TCM program targets teachers of three- to eight-year-old children. The 2014 goal is to have delivered the TCM program to 7,200 teachers, with 30 percent of these being teachers of children under five.

Conclusion

The IY TCM program is well evidenced in trials by the developer and in high-quality independent trials. It is acceptable to school-based staff and very transportable. Together with the child curriculum and parenting programs, the IY suite represents an excellent package of support for parents, children, and teachers.

What We Know

- The IY TCM program improves teacher-student relationships and home-school links, increases teacher competencies, and develops children's social and problem-solving skills.
- Strategies that maximize behavior change include a collaborative delivery style, discussion, observation of videotapes of classroom situations, role-play rehearsal, and classroom-based practice between sessions.
- The program has been shown to be effective in a variety of countries around the world.

Author's Note

The IY website has copies of most of the published studies in its library: www .incredibleyears.com.

Further information on the Welsh studies and activity in Wales can be obtained from j.hutchings@bangor.ac.uk or seen at www.incredibleyearswales.co.uk.

For information on the other studies, contact the following people:

Devon: Dr. Tamsin Ford, stars@exeter.ac.uk
Ireland: Sinead McGilloway, sinead.mcgilloway@nuim.ie
Norway: Professor Willy Tore Morch, willy-tore.morch@uit.no
Portugal: Professor Maria Filomeena Gaspar, ninigaspar@fpce.uc.pt
Jamaica: Dr. Helen Henningham, h.henningham@bangor.ac.uk
New Zealand: Lesley Stanley, Lesley.Stanley@minedu.govt.nz

About the Author

Professor **Judy Hutchings,** OBE, is director of the Centre for Evidence Based Early Intervention (CEBEI) research team at Bangor University. She undertakes research with referred children and their families and early preventive work with parents, children, and teachers.

References and Further Reading

Hutchings, J. (2012). Introducing, researching, and disseminating the Incredible Years Programmes in Wales. *International Journal of Conflict and Violence, 6*(2), 225–233.

Hutchings, J., Martin-Forbes, P., Daley, D., & Williams, M. E. (2013). A randomized controlled trial of the impact of a teacher classroom management program on the classroom behavior of children with and without behavior problems. *Journal of School Psychology, 51*(5), 571–585.

Webster-Stratton, C. (2012). *Incredible teachers: Nurturing children's social, emotional, and academic competence.* Seattle: Incredible Years, Inc.

Positive Behavioral Interventions and Supports

Catherine Bradshaw

Catherine Bradshaw describes a schoolwide framework for reducing problem behavior using positive behavior support.

Positive Behavioral Interventions and Supports (PBIS), created by Rob Horner and George Sugai, is a schoolwide application of behavioral systems and interventions to achieve behavior change in schools. PBIS has a strong foundation in behavior analysis and is a noncurricular framework that strives for a flexible fit with a school's culture and context. It can be implemented in any school level, type, or setting. A three-tiered, systemwide framework is applied that guides the development and implementation of a continuum of behavioral and academic programs and services:

- Universal (Tier 1, schoolwide "green-zone");
- Selective (Tier 2, "yellow-zone"); and
- Indicated (Tier 3, "red-zone") (see Figure 21.1).

The universal elements of the model, typically referred to as schoolwide PBIS, are the most commonly implemented aspect of the three-tiered model.

The Positive Behavioral Interventions and Supports Framework

The tiered PBIS framework focuses on the academic, behavioral, and environmental contexts in which behavior problems are observed. In applying PBIS, schools establish a set of positively stated schoolwide expectations for student behavior (e.g., "Be respectful, responsible, and ready to learn") that are developed by the

Figure 21.1   Three-Tiered Framework of Positive Behavioral Interventions and Supports

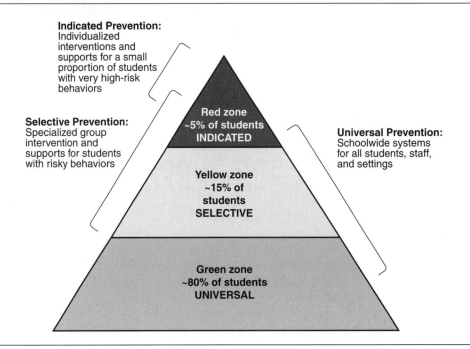

school's PBIS team and taught to all students and staff across all school settings (e.g., in the classroom, in the cafeteria, on the bus, on field trips). A schoolwide system is then developed to formalize how adults and students are recognized for exhibiting the expected positive behaviors appropriately in a given setting. Although the focus is on increasing the frequency of positive interaction between staff and students and between students themselves, tangible reinforcers, such as tickets, parties, school supplies, or special privileges, are sometimes used to formalize and prompt acknowledgments.

The PBIS framework emphasizes teaching, prompting, and acknowledging student use of developmentally and contextually appropriate expected behaviors so the following occur:

- Prosocial behaviors are more likely instead of rule-violating behavior.
- Staff attention is directed toward fostering safer and respectful school environments or cultures.
- Chaotic learning environments become more preventive, positive, and predictable.
- More strategic supports can be enlisted for students who present more resistant problem behavior.

The PBIS framework also clarifies disciplinary consequences with respect to minor (classroom-managed) and major (administrator-involved) rule violations. The school discipline system is reconceptualized as an inhibitor for students who have relatively good social behaviors and as a screening tool for students who require more intensive behavior supports and interventions.

Because student and adult behavior are so inextricably intertwined, the PBIS framework provides structures and routines to support adults so that consistency, predictability, and positive relations are promoted across school contexts. Schoolwide implementation is emphasized in order to establish staff buy-in and is facilitated through a team-based process. Each PBIS school forms a leadership or implementation team comprising a teacher from each grade level, at least one administrator, and student support staff. Parent and student membership and participation are strongly encouraged.

The PBIS team leader is often an administrator or experienced teacher. A coaching process is used at the school level and above to serve as a bridge between professional development and planning activities and the team's actual implementation efforts in the school. Coaching is also used to promote high-fidelity implementation through ongoing progress monitoring. Individuals who provide coaching supports can be internal to the school or externally provided by the district; coaches are typically school psychologists, guidance counselors, social workers, or other staff who have expertise in behavior management, data-based decision making, PBIS, and functional behavioral assessment. A district- and state-level support team is also formed to provide training, coaching, evaluation, policy, and funding guidance and technical assistance.

A critical element of the PBIS framework is the use of data to inform and guide decisions about planning and implementation. The emphasis is on the collection of multiple data elements on both desired and problem behaviors to monitor implementation quality and program outcomes. The school's PBIS team does the following:

- Specifies the most important questions that must be examined on a routine basis (e.g., rate of suspension events each day, by location, by event type)
- Determines the best data source (e.g., office discipline referrals)
- Acquires a data system that enables easy input and output displays (e.g., Schoolwide Information System [SWIS; www.swis.org])
- Follows a regular schedule for the review and analysis of data
- Develops a routine for disseminating and acting on the decisions (e.g., whole school, groups of students, and/or individual students)

Within a PBIS framework, data are used to answer four main questions:

1. How are students doing? *What's going on?*

2. Is the intervention or practice having the desired effect? *Is it working?*

3. Is the intervention being implemented as developed and recommended? *Are we using it correctly?*

4. What changes are needed to improve the effectiveness, efficiency, relevance, and durability of the intervention and its effects? *What's next?*

Does It Work?

Increasing evidence suggests that successful implementation of the schoolwide or universal PBIS system is associated with sustainable changes in disciplinary practices and improved classroom management and systems to promote positive behavior among students. Quality implementation of schoolwide PBIS has been linked with significant reductions in disruptive behaviors and improved social skills. Specifically, several studies, including two randomized controlled trials (RCTs) of schoolwide PBIS in elementary schools, have shown that implementation of the model is associated with significant reductions in office discipline referrals and suspensions and other problem behavior, such as teacher ratings of classroom behavior problems, concentration problems, and bullying, as well as improvements in emotion regulation and prosocial behavior.

Significant improvements have also been observed in student reports of school climate, staff reports of the school's organizational health (e.g., principal leadership, teacher affiliation, and academic emphasis), teacher self-efficacy, and academic achievement. The improvements in the school's organizational context achieved through PBIS may in turn enhance the implementation quality of other more intensive preventive interventions and reduce the need for more intensive school-based services.

Consistent with the three-tiered logic, evidence indicates that the impact of PBIS may vary as a function of the child's risk profile or the age at which he or she is first introduced to a PBIS environment. In a recent RCT of PBIS, in which the universal schoolwide PBIS model was contrasted with the integration of selective preventive interventions and schoolwide PBIS, significant impacts were demonstrated on teacher efficacy, academic performance, and the use of special education services. The PBIS model can be integrated with other programs, such as social-emotional learning curricula, to further enhance the impact of the tiered framework on a broader set of internalizing, externalizing, prosocial, and academic outcomes. Similar integration efforts have been initiated to successfully improve school climate and reduce bullying.

Dissemination of Positive Behavioral Interventions and Supports

Currently, more than 22,000 schools have participated in the implementation of the universal schoolwide elements of PBIS. More than forty states are working to scale up PBIS. For example, Maryland has created an extensive network of training, professional development, implementation, and evaluation supports. The national dissemination effort is led by the National Technical Assistance Center on PBIS. Recent findings from Maryland's scale-up effort indicate that high-fidelity implementation of the universal PBIS model is associated with significant effects on suspensions, academic performance, and truancy. Several state policies and some proposed federal legislation encourage the use of the three-tiered PBIS multitiered system of support framework for addressing behavior problems and promoting conditions for learning. More information on PBIS can be found at www.pbis.org.

What We Know

- Applying PBIS helps schools to establish a set of positively stated schoolwide expectations for student behavior.
- RCTs have shown that high-quality implementation of PBIS is associated with significant reductions in disruptive behaviors and improved social skills.
- The PBIS model can be integrated with other programs, such as social-emotional learning, to further enhance the impact of the tiered framework on a broader set of internalizing, externalizing, prosocial, and academic outcomes.
- The improvements in the schools' organizational context achieved through PBIS may enhance the implementation quality of other preventive interventions and reduce the need for more intensive school-based services.

About the Author

Catherine Bradshaw, PhD, MEd, is a professor and the associate dean for research and faculty development at the Curry School of Education at the University of Virginia and is the deputy director of the Johns Hopkins Center for the Prevention of Youth Violence and codirector of the Johns Hopkins Center for Prevention and Early Intervention. She conducts research on PBIS and collaborates on the scale-up of PBIS in Maryland.

References and Further Reading

Bradshaw, C. P. (2013). Preventing bullying through Positive Behavioral Interventions and Supports (PBIS): A multitiered approach to prevention and integration. *Theory Into Practice, 52*(4), 288–295.

Bradshaw, C. P., Koth, C. W., Thornton, L. A., & Leaf, P. J. (2009). Altering school climate through school-wide Positive Behavioral Interventions and Supports: Findings from a group-randomized effectiveness trial. *Prevention Science, 10*(2), 100–115.

Bradshaw, C. P., Mitchell, M. M., & Leaf, P. J. (2010). Examining the effects of school-wide positive behavioral interventions and supports on student outcomes: Results from a randomized controlled effectiveness trial in elementary schools. *Journal of Positive Behavior Interventions, 12,* 133–148.

Bradshaw, C. P., & Pas, E. T. (2011). A state-wide scale-up of Positive Behavioral Interventions and Supports (PBIS): A description of the development of systems of support and analysis of adoption and implementation. *School Psychology Review, 40,* 530–548.

Bradshaw, C. P., Waasdorp, T. E., & Leaf, P. J. (2012). Effects of school-wide Positive Behavioral Interventions and Supports on child behavior problems. *Pediatrics, 130*(5), e1136–e1145.

Horner, R. H., Sugai, G., & Anderson, C. M. (2010). Examining the evidence base for school-wide positive behavior support. *Focus on Exceptional Children, 42*(8), 1–14.

Sugai, G., & Horner, R. (2006). A promising approach for expanding and sustaining the implementation of school-wide positive behavior support. *School Psychology Review, 35,* 245–259.

Waasdorp, T. E., Bradshaw, C. P., & Leaf, P. J. (2012). The impact of School-wide Positive Behavioral Interventions and Supports (SWPBIS) on bullying and peer rejection: A randomized controlled effectiveness trial. *Archives of Pediatrics and Adolescent Medicine, 116*(2), 149–156.

First Step to Success for Preschool Children

Edward Feil, Andy Frey, and Annemieke Golly

> **Edward Feil, Andy Frey,** and **Annemieke Golly** explain how a collaborative home and school intervention program can be adapted to help young children already at risk of school failure.

The number of children displaying challenging behaviors in preschools has increased in ways that severely stress the management skills of their teachers. This has emerged as a national problem that is found widely in preschools across the United States and United Kingdom.

The purpose of this chapter is to highlight an evidence-based practice—the preschool version of First Step to Success (FS)—for young children at risk of school failure due to early signs of challenging behavior. To date, this preschool version has been implemented and evaluated in several U.S. states, including Oregon, Kentucky, and Hawaii. Herein, we first describe the K–3 FS intervention, followed by the rationale for and description of the adaptation for preschool-age children in center-based programs.

First Step to Success

FS is a collaborative home and school intervention to help at-risk students get off to a good start in school. It focuses on children who have difficulty adjusting to routine school demands. The teacher, the child's parents, and the FS coach work together to teach the child school success skills, such as following directions, doing one's work, and getting along with peers.

The three components of FS (screening, classroom, and home) require approximately three months to implement and are coordinated by a coach (i.e., behavior consultant, counselor, or early intervention specialist). The FS program is implemented in regular K–3 classrooms and is applied as part of the regular classroom teacher's classroom routines. The FS intervention teaches the following school success skills to focus children in both school and home settings:

- Communication
- Cooperation
- Limit setting
- Problem solving
- Friendship making
- Confidence building

The role of the FS coach is to teach prosocial skills to the child. One-on-one role-play and a green and red feedback card are used. The role of the focus child is to learn and master the skills. The role of the teacher is to continue teaching the skills and to recognize and praise them. The role of the parents is to teach and strengthen the skills.

Research results show that the FS program improves social skills as well as school success skills and also reduces problem behavior. FS receives high consumer satisfaction ratings from participants.

Rationale for Preschool Version

The FS intervention for younger children was modified for several reasons. Often, children come to preschool not consistently displaying knowledge of such school expectations as walking into the classroom quietly, sitting in a circle, asking for help appropriately, and so on. Many teachers believe that these behaviors do not need to be specifically taught, but they do! Lastly, teachers (from preschool through high school) too often use negative attention to mitigate students' inappropriate behavior and inadvertently exacerbate and make the challenging behavior more resistant to change.

Preschool Adaptations

During FS preschool feasibility testing, we made a number of changes and adaptations to address the specific needs of preschool children. These changes were built into the final version of the preschool FS program to increase its efficacy with preschool populations. The following adaptations were made in the FS school component:

Classroom Management Training

All teachers received training on general classroom management strategies, organized around the five universal principles of positive behavior support (PBS) that are central to FS:

1. Establish clear expectations.

2. Teach the expectations.

3. Reinforce the expectations.

4. Minimize attention for minor inappropriate behaviors.

5. Deliver clear consequences for unacceptable behavior.

Practice the Universal Principles With the Entire Class

We created small green and red cards to use with the entire class before the coach starts working with the focus student. The FS coach initially models the key universal principles for the teacher. The children receive the cards and act as "the teacher" during role-play scenarios—holding up the green card when their teachers or peers follow an expectation and red when they do not.

Additional Support for the Focus Child

Many preschool children require additional practice to master skills. As a result, the coach role-plays with the focus child before each implementation session. In the preschool version, the coach problem-solves more during the intervention than is recommended with the regular program. For example, if the child was inappropriate and did not respond to the red card, the coach asked, "Do you know why the card is on red?" If the child didn't respond, the coach said, "You need to. . ." If the child didn't respond, the coach immediately role-plays the expected behavior or target skill one-to-one in a quiet place and encourages the focus child to keep the card on green. In the original program, the coach usually keeps the card on red and the natural consequence is that the child doesn't earn points until the card goes back on green. During the first few days of the teacher phase, the coach monitors and stays in close contact with the teacher and the coach supervisor.

To remind the adults in the classroom to notice the focus child doing the right thing, we created a green badge. When the teacher phase starts, the focus student gets a green "smiley face" badge. Each day, the focus child wears this badge, which helps the adults to notice the focus student and provide specific feedback for positive behavior. Finally, many preschool children require an individual reward as well as a group reward for meeting behavioral goals during the FS intervention. The group reward, earned for the whole class by the focus child, is needed to keep peers involved, motivated, and providing peer support for the focus student. These modifications often result in a longer coach phase (ten days) compared to the elementary version (five days).

Additional Peer Support

In some cases, the focus student presents a green badge daily to another student who was especially kind and helpful. Eventually the entire class becomes part of the "green badge club"!

Adaptations to the homeBase Component

Coaches are encouraged to conduct the homeBase meetings while the child is present. The coach models positive interactions with the child and demonstrates for parents how to do the homeBase activities. Parents seem to enjoy seeing another adult treat their child with respect and interact positively with them.

Timing of the Home Component

In the K–3 FS version, the home component begins after day ten, but many parents want to begin earlier. In the preschool version, the home component starts after day three.

Child Participation

In the preschool version, we recommend that the focus child be present during the home visit. If the child cannot be present, the coach is encouraged to role-play with the parent as if the parent were the child and the coach were the parent. This type of role-play teaches the parent in a respectful, non-embarrassing way how to positively interact and play with his or her child.

Conclusion

The adapted version of the FS program provides preschool teachers with a proven intervention option that will produce the following benefits:

- Reduce behavior problems such as aggression, noncompliance, and other indicators of emerging antisocial behavior
- Substantially improve school readiness
- Improve the child's interactions and critically important relationships with the key social agents of parents and caregivers, teachers, and peers

What We Know

- FS is a collaborative home and school intervention to help at-risk students get off to a good start in school.
- FS improves social skills as well as school success skills and also reduces problem behavior.
- The adapted version of the FS program focuses on preschool children who may have difficulty adjusting to routine school demands and teaches them the expectations for behavior such as walking into the classroom quietly, sitting in a circle, and asking for help appropriately.

About the Authors

Edward Feil and **Annemieke Golly** are research scientists at Oregon Research Institute and codevelopers of the FS intervention. **Andy Frey** is a professor at the University of Louisville.

References and Further Reading

First Step to Success. Retrieved from www.firststeptosuccess.org

Sugai, G., & Horner, R. H. (2002). Introduction to positive behavioral supports in the schools [Special issue]. *Journal of Emotional and Behavioral Disorders, 10,* 130–135.

Walker, H. M., Golly, A., Kavanagh, K., Stiller, B., Severson, H. H., & Feil, E. G. (2001). *First Step to Success: Preschool edition, helping young children overcome antisocial behavior.* Longmont, CO: Sopris West, Inc.

Walker, H. M., Kavanagh, K., Stiller, B., Golly, A., Severson, H. H., & Feil, E. G. (1998). First Step to Success: An early intervention approach for preventing school antisocial behavior. *Journal of Emotional & Behavioral Disorders, 6,* 66–81.

Webster-Stratton, C., Reid, J., & Hammond, M. (2001). Preventing conduct problems, promoting social competence: A parent and teacher training partnership in Head Start. *Journal of Clinical Child Psychology, 30,* 283–302.

Improving Teaching in Science and Mathematics

Claudia Fischer and Karen Rieck

Claudia Fischer and **Karen Rieck** *report on their experiences with a German professional development program.*

Teaching aims to improve students' competencies and to help them reach and exceed their full potential in a certain domain. Teachers have to ensure that the process of competence development is effective. The reality in German classrooms has not yet reached these objectives, as international comparative studies such as Trends in International Mathematics and Science Study (TIMSS), Programme for International Student Assessment (PISA), and Progress in International Reading Literacy Study (PIRLS) have indicated. The TIMSS Video Study showed that German teachers were not aware of the central problems of classroom instruction, could not easily deal with the heterogeneity of their students, relied on a small repertoire of teaching methods, and had problems in correctly assessing student outcomes. For this reason, in 1998, the SINUS program (Increasing Efficiency in Mathematics and Science Education) was launched in Germany, addressing groups of teachers in individual schools. The program was meant to help improve actual teaching.

The SINUS Professional Development Program in Germany

SINUS was a long-term professional development initiative designed under the perspective of situated learning and was implemented on a large scale. The focus was on mathematics and science teaching. Initially intended for high schools (1998–2007), the program was adapted for elementary schools (2004–2013). About 850 elementary schools and 5,500 teachers were involved.

In accordance with Desimone (2009) and other authors, an effective training program must do the following:

- Be content based.
- Provide opportunities for active learning.
- Be closely linked to teaching and be oriented toward professional practice.
- Enhance cooperation and collaboration.
- Have a long duration.

All these elements were included in the SINUS programs.

Aims

SINUS addressed teachers as the experts in teaching and learning. Over the course of several years they worked on empirically proven central content area modules (see Figure 23.1) and thereby improved their knowledge and skills and changed their attitudes. This procedure was meant to bring innovation to classroom instruction. Finally, via modified instruction, the training aimed to enhance student motivation, interest, and learning outcomes (see Figure 23.2).

Figure 23.1 Content Areas in SINUS Describing Typical Problems in Professional Development

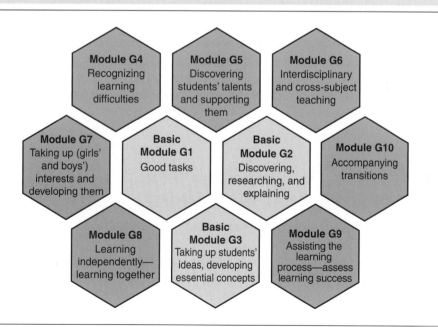

Source: Leibniz Institute for Science and Mathematics Education (IPN).

Figure 23.2 Model of Professional Development

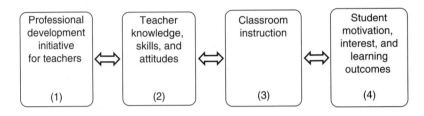

Sources: Based on Guskey (1994); Garet, Porter, Desimone, Birman, and Yoon (2001); and Desimone (2009).

Program Evaluation

The evaluation covered the four areas of the previous model:

1. How well was the program accepted?

2. Which changes could be seen in the domain of teachers' knowledge, skills, and attitudes? Which interventions supported the process of professional development?

3. What were the specific characteristics of classroom instruction in SINUS classes? How did teachers proceed while they improved teaching?

4. What about students' learning outcomes?

A series of studies was designed to monitor the program (see Figure 23.3) using instruments such as tests, surveys, videos, and files. The studies were based on mixed methods and included cross-section and panel-analyses, compared within groups and with control groups. Data from different studies were combined to obtain more reliable and valid results.

Preliminary Results

I. Professional Development Initiative for Teachers

- Teachers and principals accepted the program, understood its objectives, and felt comfortable with the procedures.
- They worked very much in line with the program and concentrated on mathematics (more) and science (less) in a problem-oriented way.
- Teachers felt supported by the specific SINUS in-service training program.
- They had little additional work due to the program.
- The longer they took part in the program, the stronger they felt the program's impact to be.

Figure 23.3 Scientific Studies Monitoring SINUS for Elementary Schools

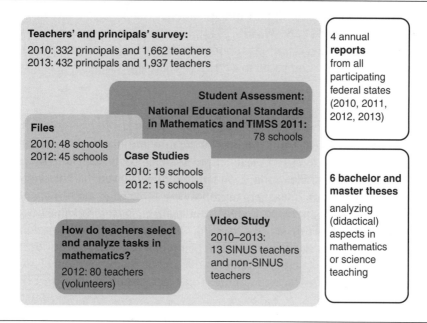

Teachers' and principals' survey:
2010: 332 principals and 1,662 teachers
2013: 432 principals and 1,937 teachers

Student Assessment:
National Educational Standards
in Mathematics and TIMSS 2011:
78 schools

Files
2010: 48 schools
2012: 45 schools

Case Studies
2010: 19 schools
2012: 15 schools

How do teachers select
and analyze tasks in
mathematics?
2012: 80 teachers
(volunteers)

Video Study
2010–2013:
13 SINUS teachers
and non-SINUS
teachers

4 annual
reports
from all
participating
federal states
(2010, 2011,
2012, 2013)

6 bachelor and
master theses
analyzing
(didactical)
aspects in
mathematics
or science
teaching

Source: Leibniz Institute for Science and Mathematics Education (IPN).

2. Teacher Knowledge, Skills, and Attitudes

- Teachers reported gaining more and deeper knowledge in mathematics and science.
- This was also true for new teaching methods and diagnostic competencies.
- The program provided competencies for more in-depth reflections on student learning.
- Reflections evolved and became more structured.
- Teachers cooperated professionally as required by the program; their cooperation mostly passed the level of exchange of teaching material and reached the levels of division of work and co-construction.

3. Classroom Instruction

- Teachers selected mathematics tasks in accordance with the national educational standards.
- They taught more science subjects than they did before the program.
- They taught science subjects in accordance with the national education standards for secondary level.
- They reflected more precisely and intensively on their own work as well as on teaching and learning processes in the classroom.
- They adopted alternative and new procedures in classroom instruction.

4. Student Motivation, Interest, and Learning Outcomes

- There were 1,581 grade four students (normally age ten) from seventy-eight SINUS schools who took part in the National Assessment of Achievement in Mathematics (2011) and TIMSS 2011.
- SINUS students' acceleration is about one-third of a school year in both mathematics and science compared to a control group of students from other schools.

Conclusion

The SINUS program for the improvement of science and mathematics teaching can serve as an example of a long-term teacher professional development initiative based on a perspective of situated learning. Evaluation results showed that the program was well accepted and supported teachers in improving knowledge and skills and evolving attitudes. The results also indicated relevant changes in classroom instruction and a clearer focus on supporting student learning. The assessment of student outcomes showed significant gains in SINUS students compared to others.

What We Know

- Professional development is a permanent social and individual need.
- Long-term initiatives based on a perspective of situated learning and working in a problem-oriented way show positive effects in the domain of teacher knowledge, skills, and attitudes.
- There is evidence for changes in classroom instruction.
- The assessment of students' outcomes showed significant gains compared to students from other schools.
- Nonetheless, more evidence is needed on the measured effects of such programs on student learning.

Authors' Note

For more information, please see the SINUS program website: www.sinus-an-grundschulen .de/index.php?id=510

About the Authors

Claudia Fischer and **Karen Rieck** work for the central coordination office of the model program *SINUS an Grundschulen* (SINUS for elementary schools) at the Leibniz Institute for Science and Mathematics Education (IPN) at the University of Kiel, Germany. Claudia Fischer is the central coordinator and is responsible for the scientific research program. Karen Rieck is the coordinator of science learning and teaching.

References and Further Reading

Dalehefte, I. M., Wendt, H., Köller, O., Wagner, H., Pietsch. M., Döring, B., Fischer, C., & Bos, W. (2014). Bilanz von neun Jahren SINUS an Grundschulen in Deutschland. Evaluation der mathematikbezogenen Daten im Rahmen von TIMSS 2011. *Zeitschrift für Pädagogik, 60*(2), 245–263.

Desimone, L. M. (2009). Improving impact studies of teachers' professional development: Toward better conceptualizations and measures. *Educational Researcher, 38*(3), 181–199.

Garet, M. S., Porter, A. C., Desimone, L. M., Birman, B., & Yoon, K. S. (2001). What makes professional development effective? Analysis of a national sample of teachers. *American Educational Research Journal, 38*(3), 915–945.

Guskey, T. R. (1994). Results-oriented professional development: In search of an optimal mix of effective practices. *Journal of Staff Development, 15*(4), 42–50.

Prenzel, M., & Ostermeier, C. (2006). Improving mathematics and science instruction: A program for the professional development of teachers. In F. K. Oser, F. Achtenhagen, & U. Renolds (Eds.), *Competence oriented teacher training. Old research demands and new pathways* (pp. 79–96). Rotterdam: Sense Publisher.

Stigler, J. W., Gonzales, P., Kawanaka, T., Knoll, S., & Serrano, A. (1999). *The TIMSS videotape classroom study: Methods and findings from an exploratory research project on eighth-grade mathematics instruction in Germany, Japan, and the United States.* Report NCES 99–074, NCES, 1999. Retrieved from http://nces.ed.gov/pubs99/1999074.pdf

Improving Reading and Math Achievement Across a Whole District

Allen Thurston, Peter Tymms,
Christine Merrell, and Nora Conlin

Allen Thurston, Peter Tymms, Christine Merrell, and Nora Conlin consider lessons learned from a project designed to improve achievement across a whole district in the United Kingdom.

Government attempts to raise achievement through policy initiatives are often disappointing. Evidence suggests that it is hard for large-scale, top-down reform to improve student achievement. For example, despite numerous reforms in English elementary schools stemming from the introduction of the Education Reform Act in 1988–2007, including national literacy and numeracy strategies, there has been virtually no improvement in reading standards and only a small improvement in math.

Ways to achieve systematic school reform at a district level have been well researched, and four main issues appear to influence effectiveness:

- Schools have to "buy into" school reform.
- The organizational constructs and structures between the district and what is required to support schools should be aligned and interconnected.
- Capacity building needs to be seen as a core function by district managers.
- There needs to be understanding of the "defined autonomy" between the district's expectations and each school's unique circumstances.

The Fife Peer Tutoring Project has established a model that might be used to further investigate the wide-scale systematic use of school reform.

Peer Tutoring

Peer tutoring involves children helping other children learn. Students work together in pairs with one child as the tutor and another as the tutee. It is important that peer tutoring is set up so that the tutor benefits, as well as the tutee. Previous research has shown the technique to be an effective approach to learning and teaching in elementary schools, with the most positive effects reported for younger, urban, low-income, and ethnic minority students. Peer tutoring was cited as providing high impact for low cost in a recent Sutton Trust report on student premiums (see References and Further Reading).

The Fife Peer Tutoring Project

In the Fife Peer Tutoring Project, a peer tutoring intervention, was evaluated over a two-year period in 129 elementary schools in one Scottish local education authority (school district). The intervention successfully raised achievement in reading and mathematics across the whole district.

The project investigated the following key questions:

- Which works best in practice: same-age or cross-age peer tutoring?
- Is an intensive or a lighter peer tutoring approach most effective?
- Is it more beneficial for students to participate in only reading or mathematics peer tutoring, or for them to participate in both?

Design of the Study

Schools were allocated to either cross- or same-age tutoring; light or intensive tutoring; or math, reading, or math and reading in a "clustered randomized controlled trial." Nearly nine thousand eight- to ten-year-old students were involved. Interventions were implemented for a fifteen-week period per year for two consecutive years.

Pairs of children were matched on the basis of previous reading or mathematics achievement (depending on the subject being tutored). In cross-age conditions, students within classes were ordered from highest to lowest in reading/mathematics achievement. The top-achieving tutor in the older class tutored the top-achieving tutee in the younger class, and so on. In the same-age conditions, classes were ordered from highest to lowest achievement in reading/mathematics. All students above the midpoint became tutors; all below became tutees. The top-achieving tutor tutored the top-achieving tutee, and so on.

In reading, the paired reading technique involved switching between the tutor and tutee reading together and the tutee reading alone. Books chosen by pairs had to be above the independent readability level of the tutee but below that of the tutor and appropriate to their interests. This facilitated the tutor helping the tutee through the error correction process. The tutor and tutee started by reading together. The tutee signaled to read alone. Upon an error, the tutor waited four to five seconds and if the tutee did not self-correct, was corrected by the tutor. The tutee repeated the error word correctly, and the pair read together again until the tutee signaled to read alone. The tutee read alone until the next error.

In math, the intervention Duolog Mathematics involved discussion between tutor and tutee to help solve math problems. First pairs read the problem together; then the tutor would contextualize it for the tutee. The tutor would question the tutee as to how they would approach solving the problem. The tutee talked out loud as they solved the problem. Tutor and tutee checked answers and summarized the nature of learning on that problem. Finally, the tutor generalized that learning to related but new contexts.

Teachers attended two professional development sessions per year. These sessions provided overviews and demonstrations of the techniques and research design. A manual and videos to support teachers were provided for each school. Teachers were supported in developing forward plans with other teachers to implement the project. More than 250 teachers were trained in the peer tutoring techniques during the two years.

Prior to the project, and for its duration, the district had an assessment system in place (the Performance Indicators in Primary Schools [PIPS] project) provided by the Centre for Evaluation and Monitoring at Durham University that enabled the progress of students to be monitored. The assessments included group written tests of mathematics and reading.

Results and Conclusion

The analyses produced a clear conclusion. Cross-age peer tutoring stood out as positively enhancing cognitive achievement for both reading and mathematics in two differently aged cohorts—for both tutors and tutees. It suggests that the approach is robust against the vagaries of implementation. Although the impact was modest, this might be improved through attention to detail, for example, in extending or improving professional development. No other interventions had as great an impact on reading or math, and there was no real benefit to using reading and math together.

In terms of district-wide school reform in the United Kingdom, the Fife Peer Tutoring Project provided a number of important lessons. Many of these relate to the process of school reform. A feature of the project was the ability of the project team to engage with the district. The district was a partner in the research/school reform process, and professional development days were coordinated and funded in partnership with the district, with the director of education in the district introducing each event. Also important was the project team's wider engagement with principals, teachers, and parents as partners in the school reform process. Principals included the process in their individual school development plans and prioritized teacher attendance at the professional development events. Professional development events also facilitated the establishment and development of networks of teachers, who met to discuss related issues. Our perception is that the high-level involvement of the district and the professional development of teachers gave a collective purpose and shared conceptualization regarding the aims and purposes of the project.

A follow-up to the Fife project, funded by the Education Endowment Foundation, is being led by Allen Thurston, Christine Merrell, and Andy Wiggins from Durham University and will attempt to scale up peer tutoring to work in four districts in a randomized controlled trial (RCT) in ninety schools taking place over the next four years. The disparate nature of district context and wide variety of district-level support should provide fresh challenges to gauge the ability of peer tutoring to promote school reform at scale-up.

What We Know

- Cross-age peer tutoring was effective at raising achievement in reading and mathematics.
- Same-age tutoring, while easier to organize, was not effective.
- It is possible to work with schools on a wide basis on a clustered RCT.

Authors' Note

The research project was supported by a grant from the Economic and Social Research Council, Knowledge Transfer Partnerships scheme. Keith Topping and David Miller from the University of Dundee were coinvestigators on the grant.

About the Authors

Allen Thurston is professor of education and director of the Centre for Effective Education at Queen's University Belfast. He conducts work on cooperative learning in the areas of science, literacy, numeracy, and the use of RCTs in education.

Peter Tymms is a professor of education and director of the iPIPS project, Durham University. His research interests are monitoring, assessment, peer learning, attention deficit/hyperactivity disorder (ADHD), Rasch measurement, and research methodology.

Christine Merrell is the director of research at the Centre for Evaluation and Monitoring, Durham University. Her research interests are assessment development and monitoring the progress of children through primary school.

Nora Conlin is an education officer at Fife Council. Her interests include school management and school improvement and peer learning.

References and Further Reading

Higgins, S., Kokotsaki, D., & Coe, R. (2011). *Toolkit of strategies to improve learning: Summary for schools spending the pupil premium.* Durham, UK: Sutton Trust/Durham University. Retrieved from www.suttontrust.com/ research/toolkit-of-strategies-to-improvelearning/

Tymms, P., Merrell, C., Thurston, A., Andor, J., Topping, K. J., & Miller, D. J. (2011). Improving attainment across a whole district: School reform through peer tutoring in a randomized controlled trial. *School Effectiveness and School Improvement, 22*(3), 265–289.

Co-Teaching

Inclusion and Increased Student Achievement

Marilyn Friend and Tammy Barron

Co-teaching is effective in improving outcomes for children with disabilities but only when it is implemented with fidelity, say **Marilyn Friend** and **Tammy Barron**.

Co-teaching occurs when special and general educators share classroom responsibilities so that students with disabilities can access the same curriculum while receiving specialist support. Although co-teaching has been an option for educating students with disabilities for more than twenty-five years in the United States, it has recently grown in popularity, probably because professionals are increasingly recognizing that nearly all children can and should reach today's rigorous academic standards.

Co-Teaching Basics

Maximizing the potential of co-teaching depends heavily on understanding its unique features and implementing it accordingly. Overall, co-teaching occurs when a general education teacher and a special education teacher collaborate in the typical classroom, committing to educate all their class effectively. Their partnership has these characteristics:

- The teachers have parity; that is, the class is a two-teacher class rather than a one-teacher class with a talented helper assigned. However, the exact nature of each professional's roles and responsibilities depends on the grade level, subject, lesson, and teachers' specific knowledge and skills.
- The class includes a cluster of students with disabilities or other special needs, but other class members represent the majority of pupils. The

co-taught class is not a class composed mostly of children who struggle to learn.

- The co-taught class may occur for all or part of a subject (e.g., for an hour during an elementary language arts/English lesson or for the entire algebra class with fourteen- and fifteen-year-olds); in some situations, teachers partner for longer periods of time.
- The specially designed teaching that is required for students with disabilities is embedded in the overall lesson delivery.

Co-teaching is a unique educational model. Unlike team teaching, in which two general educators combine class groups and expertise (e.g., an English teacher and a history teacher blending their two classes to teach history through literature), co-teachers bring different types of expertise—equally valuable—to their lessons:

- General educators are primarily experts in their academic content, while special educators are experts in the details of how children learn and how to facilitate learning, whether in the academic, behavioral, social, or emotional domains.
- General educators typically are focused on groups of children, while special educators are oriented to think of each individual's specific characteristics and needs.
- General educators are attuned to students experiencing difficulty beyond what is typical, given the grade level and subject; special educators have extensive responsibility for documenting the specific components of a child's education, including through individualized education programs (IEPs) in the United States or in the United Kingdom if they have a statement of special educational needs.
- General educators want all their students to learn but also must keep up the teaching pace; special educators adopt a teach-to-mastery mind-set that tends to supersede pacing as the first priority.

Co-Teaching in Action

Co-taught classes are exciting places. Here are several examples of what we observe:

- One teacher leads the whole group while the other gathers data on specific children, a small group of students, or the entire class. Data may pertain to the day's lesson, inappropriate behavior, pupil participation, or any other domain the teachers decide should be considered.
- Children are working in three groups. Two are led by the teachers to address different dimensions of the day's lesson, while in the third group students independently complete a review activity or collaborate with peers on a project or assignment. All children participate in all three groups.
- Each teacher leads half of the class—sometimes covering the same material so that all students can participate more and sometimes addressing the material in different ways to facilitate diverse children's learning.
- While one teacher works with most of the class, the other selects a small group for remediation, additional practice, enrichment, pre-teaching, assessment, or any other instructional purpose.

- The teachers may sometimes function as partners with the entire class group, perhaps with one teacher introducing a concept and the other providing an example of it or one speaking while the other draws a visual representation of the information to clarify it.
- Occasionally, one teacher leads instruction while the other quietly assists individual children. This type of co-teaching is generally considered the least effective model; it should be employed only sparingly.

Implementing With Fidelity

The real benefits of co-teaching are achieved when it is implemented with fidelity within a supportive environment. Co-teaching is a sophisticated service delivery option that relies on appropriate attention to a variety of details. Unless areas such as the following are addressed, effective co-teaching implementation and sustainability are unlikely.

Commitment and Support From the Leadership

When school leaders establish clear expectations for co-teaching practice and demonstrate commitment to implementation, it flourishes. School and district (local authority) leaders should do the following:

- Believe co-teaching is imperative and purposefully support it through actions rather than just words.
- Expect teachers to collaborate to increase all students' learning.
- Hold teachers accountable for co-teaching implementation fidelity.
- Celebrate co-teaching successes and problem-solve issues that arise.
- Develop co-teaching programs by sharing leadership roles with teachers who are passionate about it.

In addition, education leaders should anticipate that co-teaching programs develop across time. They should be prepared to support initial implementation, encourage continued expansion, and resolve matters such as teacher conflict. They should also arrange professional development on pertinent topics, including collaboration skills and co-teaching strategies.

Logistics

In addition to leadership support, co-teaching requires attention to several key practical matters, the most important of which are (1) arranging common planning time and (2) creating appropriate schedules and assigning children to co-taught classes. Logistics should include the following:

- Arranging regularly scheduled common planning time
- Monitoring co-teachers' other obligations (e.g., committees) so that collaboration is feasible rather than overwhelming
- Providing electronic options for collaboration (e.g., wikis)

- Ensuring that co-taught classes include a heterogeneous mix of students at various academic levels
- Limiting the number of children with disabilities in any co-taught class to preserve class heterogeneity

Teacher Knowledge, Skills, and Commitment

Teachers should begin co-teaching with a commitment to the collaborative structure on which co-teaching is based. Next, they should possess a high level of skill in their own disciplines (that is, general education versus special education). They then create a relationship with their teacher partner in order to blend their knowledge to enhance learning. For example, use the general educator's knowledge of the science curriculum and the special educator's knowledge about teaching vocabulary and using visuals to create intensive and engaging lessons for students.

Is It Working?

Effectiveness indicators include the following:

- Many children with disabilities have higher reading and mathematics achievement than they did when educated in a special education setting.
- Students who are co-taught perceive they are members of the classroom community and feel less stigmatized.
- Co-teachers report that benefits to children include not only increased academic performance but also improved self-confidence, social skills, and peer relations.

Conclusion

Co-teaching is an exciting but complex service delivery model of teaching that holds tremendous promise for increasing the achievement of children with disabilities while ensuring that they are included in their school communities. School districts in the United States that emphasize collaboration and co-teaching achieve better academic outcomes for students with disabilities than comparable districts not using this model. When set into a context of strong beliefs in students' potential and nurtured through a collaborative school culture with clear expectations and strong administrative leadership, co-teaching can both provide access to the general curriculum and ensure that specially designed instruction is offered across the academic, social, emotional, and behavioral domains.

What We Know

- Co-teaching facilitates pupil achievement when both implemented with fidelity and incorporating specially designed teaching.

- The context for effective co-teaching is a collaborative school culture and an inclusive belief system.
- Co-teaching programs rely on strong leadership support, attention to logistics, and highly skilled professionals

About the Authors

Marilyn Friend is professor emerita of education at the University of North Carolina at Greensboro. She is also past president of the Council for Exceptional Children. She is internationally recognized for her work in the areas of collaboration, inclusive practices, and co-teaching.

Tammy Barron is a doctoral student at the University of North Carolina at Greensboro. Her research focuses on inclusive practices and co-teaching. She has co-taught at the elementary, middle, and high school levels serving children with mild to moderate disabilities.

References and Further Reading

Friend, M. (2014), *Co-teach! Creating and sustaining classroom partnerships in inclusive schools* (2nd ed.). Greensboro, NC: Marilyn Friend, Inc.

Friend, M., & Cook, L. (2013). *Interactions: Collaboration skills for school professionals* (7th ed.). Upper Saddle River, NJ: Pearson/Allyn & Bacon.

Gurgur, H., & Uzuner, Y. (2011). Examining the implementation of two co-teaching models: Team teaching and station teaching. *International Journal of Inclusive Education, 15,* 589–610.

Huberman, M., Navo, M., & Parrish, T. (2012). Effective practices in high performing districts serving students in special education. *Journal of Special Education Leadership, 25*(2), 59–71.

Walsh, J. M. (2012). Co-teaching as a school system strategy for continuous improvement. *Preventing School Failure, 56*(1), 29–36.

Implementing Response to Instruction and Intervention With Older Students

Nancy Frey and Douglas Fisher

Nancy Frey and **Douglas Fisher** explain how to deliver a multitiered system of intervention effectively.

There is a great deal of evidence about effective interventions for younger children, especially in the areas of basic literacy skills and mathematics knowledge. However, much less is known about effective systems of intervention for older students.

Multitiered Response to Intervention (RTI) systems have the potential to support older students who are struggling. RTI models usually consist of three tiers of teaching, with core Tier 1 teaching for all children, Tier 2 support for students falling below their expected level, and Tier 3 support for those at high risk of academic failure.

One such multitiered system, Response to Instruction and Intervention (RTI^2), shows promise. When correctly implemented, RTI^2 ensures that children who fail to respond to high-quality teaching are identified and that their needs are addressed. In this chapter, we focus on several of the factors necessary to implement the RTI^2 system of support effectively.

Start With Universal Screening

At the start of every year, all students are assessed to determine who might need supplemental or intensive interventions immediately. Screening tools should be quick and fairly easy to use because they are going to be administered to all students.

These tools are not expected to be diagnostic and might unintentionally identify children who really did not need an intervention. Keep in mind that a screening tool merely identifies students who are working below grade level; these tools cannot assess what approaches have been tried in the past and whether these have been successful or not. It is common to use writing, encoding (spelling) inventories, and general mathematics skills as screening tools. The U.S. National Center on Response to Intervention lists a number of formal screening tools, and these are available at www.rti4success.org/screeningTools.

Regardless of the tools used, there must be a process in place to identify children in need of further investigation and possible intervention, and those interventions should begin within the first few weeks of the school year. Simply said, if universal screening is not part of the back-to-school experience, the school is not implementing RTI².

High-Quality Tier I Instruction

The RTI² system is built on the idea that all children receive high-quality teaching. At least 75 percent of students should experience success in Tier 1, core instruction. If that is not the case, then school improvement efforts should focus on this level of instruction. At minimum, students in Tier 1 teaching should do the following:

- Know what they are expected to learn
- Have their teachers model for them
- Engage in productive group work
- Have their errors and misconceptions addressed using prompts and cues rather than direct explanations
- Be held accountable for their learning

When at least 75 percent of children in a given school are not achieving as expected or are not making progress, RTI² would suggest a systematic review of the quality of the teaching students are receiving.

Progress Monitoring

As part of Tier 1, there needs to be a system for monitoring students' progress. There will be children who do not appear to require supplemental or intensive interventions based on the screening tools but who nonetheless fail to respond to high-quality teaching. In other words, pupil progress must be monitored on a regular basis using appropriate tools. The challenge with older students is finding appropriate tools.

While there are formal tools, such as those recommended by the National Center on Response to Intervention (www.rti4success.org/progressMonitoringTools), several schools have developed their own systems for monitoring pupil progress. For example, some schools develop course competencies, or common formative assessments, that allow for an assessment of all students enrolled in a particular course.

Children who do not demonstrate competency on one of these assessments are automatically referred to the RTI^2 committee for review. Sometimes the committee reviews the situation and recommends against intervention, especially when motivation, attendance, or illness are considered. At other times, the committee recommends intervention.

The competencies serve as curriculum-based assessment, meaning that there is "direct observation and recording of a student's performance in the local curriculum as a basis for gathering information to make instructional decisions" (Deno, 1987, p. 41). These tools allow teachers to determine if children are making progress in the regular curriculum of the course.

One of the challenges to an RTI^2 effort in middle and high schools relates to the progress-monitoring systems commonly used. In many schools, students can receive supplemental and intensive interventions based only on their performance in reading or mathematics. In fact, nearly all formal progress-monitoring tools focus on reading and mathematics, meaning that other content areas are not reviewed. When teachers across the disciplines develop course competencies, progress monitoring occurs in every classroom, and every teacher becomes involved in the RTI^2 process.

Supplemental and Intensive Interventions

Identifying the need is an important aspect of a multitiered system of support, but it is not enough. Once students are identified, whether through universal screening or progress monitoring, appropriate intervention must be delivered and monitored. In an RTI^2 model, there are typically two levels of intervention: supplemental and intensive.

Supplemental interventions are those that are delivered in a small-group setting, with a group of children who have similar educational needs. Supplemental interventions occur at least three times per week for thirty minutes, but many children need more support than that. In essence, supplemental intervention focuses on students' needs and ensures that they have additional direct and guided teaching aligned with those needs.

Intensive interventions are those that are delivered individually. Like supplemental interventions, intensive interventions occur at least three times per week for thirty minutes, but many students receive daily intervention. Typically, intensive intervention is reserved for children who are significantly below grade level and focuses on basic skills and access to the core curriculum.

Both supplemental and intensive interventions need to be monitored. At minimum, assessment data should be collected every two weeks (if not weekly) for students receiving supplemental interventions and weekly (if not daily) for children receiving intensive interventions. Assessment information should be reviewed by an appropriately constructed committee—not only the individuals providing the intervention—so that trends can be identified and discussed and alternatives can be proposed.

When a given pupil fails to respond to supplemental interventions, intensive interventions can be used. When sufficient time has passed and a given pupil fails to respond to intensive interventions, the team may consider a referral for special education services. Failure to respond to high-quality instruction and supplemental and intensive interventions suggests that the pupil may need more long-term support and specialized services to be successful in school.

Conclusion

Creating and implementing a multitiered system of support, such as RTI^2, is complex but worth the effort. It is complex because systems that systematically collect and review data do not often exist, much less align interventions to those data. However, it is worth the effort because students make significant progress when they receive the support they need.

What We Know

- RTI systems have the potential to support older children who are struggling.
- At least 75 percent of RTI^2 students should experience success in Tier 1, core teaching.
- Universal screening at the beginning of the school year should identify children who might need supplemental or intensive interventions immediately.
- The progress of all students should be monitored across a range of subjects, not just reading and mathematics.

About the Authors

Nancy Frey is professor of literacy in the School of Teacher Education at San Diego State University. Previously, she was a public school teacher at the elementary and middle school level and worked for the Florida Inclusion Network helping districts design systems for supporting children with disabilities in the general education classroom.

Douglas Fisher is professor of language and literacy education in the Department of Teacher Education at San Diego State University and a classroom teacher at Health Sciences High and Middle College. He has received several awards, including the International Reading Association Celebrate Literacy Award, the Farmer award for excellence in writing from the National Council of Teachers of English, and the Christa McAuliffe Excellence in Teacher Education Award.

References and Further Reading

Deno, S. L. (1987). Curriculum-based measurement. *Teaching Exceptional Children, 20,* 41.

Fisher, D., & Frey, N. (2010). *Enhancing RTI: How to ensure success with effective classroom instruction and intervention.* Alexandria, VA: ASCD.

Fisher, D., & Frey, N. (2013). Implementing RTI in a high school: A case study. *Journal of Learning Disabilities, 46,* 99–114.

Fuchs, L. S., Fuchs, D., & Compton, D. (2010). Rethinking response to intervention at middle and high school. *School Psychology Review, 39,* 22–28.

Vaughn, S., Cirino, P. T., Wanzek, J., Wexler, J., Fletcher, J. M., Denton, C. A., & Francis, D. J. (2010). Response to Intervention for middle school students with reading difficulties: Effects of a primary and secondary intervention. *School Psychology Review, 39,* 3–21.

Teaching English Language Learners in Inclusion Settings

Kristi Santi and David Francis

Kristi Santi and **David Francis** outline best practices and explain how these can also apply to children with learning disabilities.

Schools face a challenge. How can they improve outcomes for English language learners (ELLs) and those with disabilities while avoiding negative impacts for others? Although the needs of individual children may differ, it is possible to design curricula and deliver teaching in ways that are sensitive to diverse learning needs and are cost-effective. In this chapter we focus on ELLs, but many of the key principles can be extended to other learners with special educational needs.

Learning to Read and Struggling to Read

Learning to read in English is a vital first step for ELLs in the classroom. Reading is a complex cognitive skill that is linguistically based, developmental, and acquired, by which we mean that it is a skill that is almost always learned through teaching. To say that reading is developmental implies that the process of learning to read differs from the practice of reading, once reading has been mastered, and that reading is dependent on the development of specific cognitive skills to support its acquisition. Reading is more like learning to play the piano than learning to speak one's native language.

Researchers who study reading agree that learning to read in an alphabetic language (i.e., any language that uses letters to represent sounds) follows a common developmental sequence, regardless of the language. Moreover, when reading acquisition in an alphabetic language fails, the root problem typically lies at the single-word level and arises from a breakdown in phonological processing.

Children who struggle to acquire literacy will not simply outgrow their reading problems. However, well-designed teaching can prevent many reading problems, while other problems can be ameliorated, and in some cases completely remediated, through effective intervention.

What About English Language Learners?

Children who struggle with phonological processing will struggle to acquire literacy in any alphabetic language, whether they are native speakers of that language or not. Moreover, children who struggle to acquire literacy benefit from the same types of direct, systematic, and explicit teaching in phonemic awareness, phonics, and fluency whether they are native speakers of the language or not. Although teaching may need to be adjusted to make the content accessible to nonnative speakers of a language, the process of literacy acquisition is not otherwise qualitatively different between native and nonnative speakers of the language.

However, as children mature as readers, they move beyond learning to read and instead read to learn. As children work with more complex and demanding text, fluency, background knowledge, and language skills play an increasingly important role in comprehension. Decoding skills remain important to comprehension, but differences between students in their understanding of texts are increasingly a function of what they know and their academic language skills. Recent findings from several U.S. studies highlight that many nonnative speakers of English develop average or above-average abilities in decoding but have very weak academic vocabularies and, consequently, poor reading comprehension. Core reading programs should build academic language skills through vocabulary and text comprehension, and in fact this is effective in preventing reading difficulties in all children.

Key Principles for Effective Inclusion

Cognitive and behavioral science reveals that the ways in which children learn are more similar than they are different. For example, nonnative speakers and children with learning disabilities often need more time to process information and do better when information is presented in shorter segments. They also benefit from instructional supports that activate prior knowledge, make concepts visible, and make the language more accessible. Although the source of their difficulties differs, the teaching practice that benefits the two types of learners is similar.

Focus on Instructional Activities, Not Just Instructional Materials

Previous research has shown that approaches that change instructional activities are most effective.

- Plan for diverse learners in advance. Teachers can both anticipate areas in the lesson that may pose difficulty for at-risk learners and plan to include the explicit development of vocabulary and key concepts.

- Segment lessons and provide multiple opportunities for students to engage in discourse to turn passive participants into active learners.
- New material should be taught in chunks. Teacher modeling should be followed by students practicing with peers and then simple formative assessment, such as responding on whiteboards, thumbs up-thumbs down, or seat-partner review.
- Structure and clear directions relieve anxiety and allow students to focus on learning.
- Use visual aids.
- Use students' differences and background experiences to support their academic development.
- Allow for student discourse.

Peer-Assisted Learning

A tried and tested approach to improving learning outcomes for all children comes from making them teachers as well as learners. Peer-assisted learning strategies have been employed in classrooms for more than forty years. Children work together in pairs, typically partnered based on ability (e.g., a low-performing reader is paired with an average reader), and take turns reading and asking/answering comprehension questions. These activities occur several times per week and are highly structured, with the teacher continuously monitoring responses and visiting student pairs, typically spending more time with the lower-performing pairs. The time spent engaged in reading and discussion of the content provides at-risk children with multiple opportunities and ample time to process, learn, and organize material in a way that matches their needs. Although this technique is most widely known in early reading, it has also been proven to be effective in mathematics and with older students. Peer-assisted learning promotes the academic success of all learners (i.e., it is not detrimental to high achievers).

Use of Assessment Data to Inform Teaching

Assessment provides a tool for monitoring progress, can identify those students who are struggling, and motivate those at risk. Teachers who use formative assessment on a daily basis are better able to adapt their lessons to meet the needs of all learners.

- At the start of each unit an assessment should determine knowledge of core concepts and vocabulary. This can also be used to group children for peer-assisted learning or small-group teaching.
- At the start of each lesson, effective teachers assess prior learning. These activities are quick—taking on average no more than three to four minutes—and help connect the new learning to past learning. Children quickly understand that learning is not an isolated, one-day event, but fulfills a larger purpose to be built up throughout the year.
- During lessons, teachers embed checks for understanding that also allow them to evaluate lesson pacing.
- Lessons end with a determination of learning—a quick check to assess what has been learned from the lesson of the day.

Conclusion

We have shown how children from diverse backgrounds at risk for reading failure ben-efit from similar teaching when the teaching is supported to make it accessible. Effective classroom teaching can allow ELLs—and other at-risk students—to thrive in inclusive settings. Furthermore, it can actually prevent the development of learning disabilities.

We reviewed several characteristics of effective teaching focusing on activities that (1) make children active participants in their learning, (2) develop students' mastery of academic language, (3) engage peers in the learning and teaching, and (4) use assessment to measure learning and adjust teaching. Specific routes to changing teaching in these ways hold significant promise for creating a better educational system for an increasingly diverse population of learners.

What We Know

- Children who struggle with phonological processing will struggle to acquire literacy in any alphabetic language.
- Core reading programs can be effective in preventing reading difficulties in all students.
- Changing teaching methods and using data to inform teaching will benefit ELLs and children with learning disabilities.

About the Authors

Kristi Santi is associate professor of special education at the University of Houston, focusing on reading instruction and assessment and English language learners with and without disabilities. She is also a professional development trainer and previously worked as a special education teacher.

David Francis is the Hugh Roy and Lillie Cranz Cullen Professor and chairman of the Department of Psychology at the University of Houston. His areas of interest include reading acquisition and the early identification and prevention of reading disabilities, developmental disabilities, and psychometrics.

References and Further Reading

Bergsmann, E. M., Lüftenegger, M., Jöstl, G., Schober, B., & Spiel, C. (2013). The role of classroom structure in fostering students' school functioning: A comprehensive and application-oriented approach. *Learning and Individual Differences, 26,* 131–138.

Branum-Martin, L., Mehta, P. D., Fletcher, J. M., Carlson, C. D., Ortiz, A., Carlo, M., & Francis, D. J. (2006). Bilingual phonological awareness: Multilevel construct validation among Spanish-speaking kindergarteners in transitional bilingual education classrooms. *Journal of Educational Psychology, 98*(1), 170–181.

Center on Instruction at RMC Research Corporation. Retrieved from www .centeroninstruction.org

Cheung, A., & Slavin, R. E. (2005). Effective reading programs for English language learners and other language-minority students. *Bilingual Research Journal, 29*, 241–267.

Clark, R. C., Kirschner, P. A., & Sweller, J. (2012). Putting students on the path to learning: The case for fully guided instruction. *American Educator, 36*(1), 6–11.

The IRIS Center Peabody College Vanderbilt University. Retrieved from iriscenter. com/index.html

Lesaux, N. (2012). Reading and reading instruction for children from low-income and non-English-speaking households. *The Future of Children, 22,* 73–88.

Slavin, R. E., Cheung, A., Groff, C., & Lake, C. (2008). Effective reading programs for middle and high schools: A best-evidence synthesis. *Reading Research Quarterly, 43,* 290–322.

Vaughn, S., Cirino, P. T., Tolar, T., Fletcher, J. M., Cardenas-Hagan, E., Carlson, C. D., & Francis, D. J. (2008). Long-term follow-up of Spanish and English interventions for first-grade English language learners at risk for reading problems. *Journal of Research on Educational Effectiveness, 1,* 179–214.

Ziegler, J. C., & Goswami, U. (2005). Reading acquisition, developmental dyslexia, and skilled reading across languages: A psycholinguistic grain size theory. *Psychological Bulletin, 131*(1), 3–29.

Index

Academic engagement, 85
Accountability
    co-teaching programs, 123
    England–Wales educational performance
        comparisons, 45–48, 46 (figure)
    formative assessment, 12
    large-scale assessments, 26–27, 30–31, 32
    tiered intervention programs, 127
Active learning, 62, 73, 132–133
Affective engagement, 86
Ager, R., 49
Alberto, P. A., 93
Almond, R. G., 44
American Psychological Association (APA), 64
Anderson, C. M., 104
Anderson, L., 63, 64
Andor, J., 120
Andrade, H., 23, 24
Andrews, D., 53
Appleton, J. J., 89
Applied behavioral analysis (ABA), 62, 90–93
Appropriate conduct, 63
Arter, J. A., 5, 27, 28
Assessment for learning, 12
Assessment practices
    balanced assessments, 25–28
    differentiated classrooms, 1–4
    diverse learners, 133
    England–Wales educational performance
        comparisons, 45–48
    feedback, 11–12, 13–14 (table), 14, 36–37
    high-stakes assessments, 39–43, 47–48
    large-scale assessments, 26–27, 30–31
    multiple measures strategies, 16–19, 31
Atkinson, A., 49
At-risk students, 105–108, 132
    see also English language learners (ELLs)
Attention, 63, 68
Axelrod, S., 93

Baker-Henningham, Helen, 96
Balanced assessments, 25–28
BBC News, 49
Bear, G. G., 61
Behavioral engagement, 86
Behavioral, Instructional, and Organizational
        (BIO) classroom management
        approach
    see Consistency Management & Cooperative
        Discipline (CMCD)
Behavior management
    Consistency Management & Cooperative
        Discipline (CMCD) model, 80–83,
        82 (table)
    effective classroom management practices,
        62, 76–78
    First Step to Success (FS) program, 105–108
    Incredible Years (IY) Teacher Classroom
        Management (TCM) program, 94–97
    Positive Behavioral Interventions and
        Supports (PBIS) model, 99–103,
        100 (figure)
    positive reinforcement practices, 90–93
Bergsmann, E. M., 134
Bernhardt, V. L., 19
Berry, B., 93
Best Evidence Encyclopedia (BEE), 50, 57
Better: Evidence-Based Education, ix, xi
Birman, B., 112 (figure), 115
Bjork, R., 55, 59
Black, P., 5, 15, 26, 29, 38
Bos, W., 115
Bradshaw, C. P., 103, 104
Bradshaw, J., 49
Branum-Martin, L., 134
Brief constructed response (BCR) tests, 31
Brookhart, S. M., 19
Burge, B., 49
Burgess, S., 48, 49

Cameron, C., 24
Capacity building, 87, 116
Cardenas-Hagan, E., 135
Caring behaviors, 81
Carlo, M., 134
Carlson, C. D., 134, 135
Center for Advancement of Learning and
    Assessment, 39
Center for Research and Reform in Education,
    ix, xi
Center on Instruction at RMC Research
    Corporation, 135
Centre for Evaluation and Monitoring, 118
Chappuis, J., 5
Chappuis, S., 5
Charles, C. M., 70
Check & Connect on What
    Works Clearinghouse, 89
Check & Connect program, 85–88
Checklists, 21–22, 93
Cheung, A., 135
Chi, M. T. H., 44
Choice, 56
Christenson, S. L., 89
Cirino, P. T., 130, 135
Cizek, G., 23
Clark, R. C., 135
Classroom assessments, 25, 26
Classroom climate, 37
Classroom Dinosaur School program, 94–97
Classroom management practices
    basic principles, 61–62
    challenges, 71, 74, 76–78, 90
    Consistency Management & Cooperative
        Discipline (CMCD) model, 80–83,
        82 (table)
    developmental differences, 63–64
    disciplinary actions, 61, 69, 77
    effectiveness, 62, 66–67
    First Step to Success (FS) program, 105–108
    Incredible Years (IY) Teacher Classroom
        Management (TCM) program, 94–97
    positive reinforcement practices, 90–93
    professional collaborations, 71–72, 74
    purpose and characteristics, 60–61
    relevant research, 72, 78, 83, 87
    tiered intervention programs, 61, 99–103,
        100 (figure)
    timing considerations, 62–63, 67–69
    training opportunities, 73–74, 79, 110–114
    see also Behavior management
Classroom Organization and Management
    Program (COMP), 73–74, 75

Coaching practices, 101
Coe, R., 15, 120
Cognitive engagement, 86
Cognitive processes, 41
Coleman, R., 15
Collaborative environments, 71–72, 74
Collaborative home and school interventions
    see First Step to Success (FS)
Commercially-based assessment
    see Interim assessments
Common Core State Standards, 30, 56
Community involvement, 82
Compensatory assessment, 18
Complementary assessment, 18
Compliments, 91–92
Compton, D., 130
Conduct, appropriate, 63
Consistency, 87
Consistency Management & Cooperative
        Discipline (CMCD), 80–83, 82 (table)
Content-specific tests, 31
Continuity, 87
Cook, L., 125
Cooperative discipline, 81
Cooper, J. O., 93
Cost-benefit analysis, 51–53, 52 (table)
Co-teaching programs
    basic concepts, 121–122
    effectiveness, 124–125
    instructional practices, 122–123
    leadership support, 123
    logistics, 123–124
    teacher commitment, 124
Crone, D. H., 64
Cross-age peer tutoring, 117–119
Croxson, B., 49

Dalehefte, I. M., 115
Daley, D., 98
Data-driven decisions, 50
Data-informed instructional planning, 2–3
Davies, A., 24
Deakin-Crick, R., 15
Decision-making challenges, 56–57
Declarative knowledge, 41, 42
DeNisi, A., 15
Deno, S. L., 130
Denton, C. A., 130
Desimone, L. M., 111, 112 (figure), 115
Devon, 95
Differentiated instruction, 1–4
Direct costs, 51
Disabled students, 121–125, 132, 134

Disciplinary practices
  see Behavior management; Classroom
      management practices
Diverse learners, 131–134
Döring, B., 115
Driscoll, A., 84
Du, Y., 24
Duolog Mathematics, 118
Durham University, 118, 119
Dweck, C., 3, 5

Earl, L., 5
Education Endowment Foundation, 119
Education Reform Act, 116
Effective educational practices, 55–58, 66–67
Elementary school level, 63–64, 110–114,
      113 (figure), 117–119
Emmer, E., 61, 63, 64, 65, 70
Engagement, student, 73, 85–86
England–Wales educational performance
      comparisons, 45–48, 46 (figure)
English language learners (ELLs)
  instructional practices, 131–134
  summative assessment, 4
EPPI-Centre, 57
Error analysis, 8–9, 9 (figure)
Evertson, C., 60, 63, 64, 65, 70, 72, 75
Evidence-based educational practices, 50–53,
      56–58, 78
  see also Check & Connect program;
      Incredible Years (IY) Teacher Classroom
      Management (TCM) program

Federal Trade Commission (FTC), 55
Feedback
  benefits, 14
  characteristics, 12, 13–14 (table)
  formative assessment, 3, 8, 11–12,
      13–14 (table), 14, 36–37
  multiple measures strategies, 17, 31
  self-assessment strategies, 20–23, 36–37
Feed-forward strategy, 8–10
Feil, E. G., 109
Fidelity, 51–53, 123–124
Fife Peer Tutoring Project, 116, 117–119
First Step to Success (FS), 105–108, 109
Fisher, D., 10, 130
Fleischman, S., 58
Fletcher, J. M., 130, 134, 135
Florida State University, 39
Focus child
  see First Step to Success (FS)
Formal assessments, 3

Formative assessment
  benefits, 6
  characteristics, 7 (figure)
  classroom assessments, 26
  classroom climate, 37
  differentiated classrooms, 2–3
  diverse learners, 133
  error analysis, 8–9, 9 (figure)
  feedback, 3, 8, 11–12, 13–14 (table), 14, 36–37
  feed-forward strategy, 8–10
  high schools, 6–10
  multiple measures strategies, 17, 18–19
  purpose, 6–7, 35, 37–38
  self-assessment strategies, 20, 36–37
  students' role, 36–37
  student understanding checks, 7–8
  teacher's role, 35–36
Francis, D. J., 130, 134, 135
Freiberg, H. J., 82 (table), 84
Frey, N., 10, 130
Friend, M., 125
Fuchs, D., 130
Fuchs, L. S., 130
Furlong, M. J., 89

Garet, M. S., 112 (figure), 115
General Certificate of Secondary Education
      (GCSE), 45
Germany, 110–114
Gibbons, S., 49
Golly, A., 109
Gonzales, P., 115
Good, T., 72, 75
Goswami, U., 135
Gregory, K., 24
Groff, C., 135
Group work, 66–67
Growth mind-set, 3
Gurgur, H., 125
Guskey, T. R., 112 (figure), 115

Hammond, M., 109
Hansen, B.A., 56, 59
Harlen, W., 15
Harrison, C., 15
Hattie, J., 10, 12, 14 (table), 15, 38
Hawken, L. S., 64
Hawkins, K., 44
Heath, C., 56, 58
Heath, D., 56, 58
Helton, S., 84
Heritage, M., 29
Heron, T. E., 93

Heward, W. L., 93
Higgins, S., 15, 120
High-quality Tier 1 instruction, 127
High school students, 6–10
High-stakes assessment, 39–43, 47–48
Home and school collaborative interventions
    see First Step to Success (FS)
HomeBase meetings, 108
Horner, R. H., 64, 99, 104, 109
Huberman, M., 125
Hutchings, J., 98
Huzinec, C. A., 84

Inattention, 63
Increasing Efficiency in Mathematics and
    Science Education
    see SINUS professional development program
        (Increasing Efficiency in Mathematics
        and Science Education)
Incredible Years (IY) Teacher Classroom
    Management (TCM) program, 94–97
Indicated prevention programs, 61, 99–103,
    100 (figure)
Indirect costs, 51
Individualized interventions, 61
Informal assessments, 3
In-service training, 73, 79
Institute for Effective Education, ix, xi
Institute of Education Sciences (IES), 43
Institute of Medicine, 89
Instructional organization, 82
Intensive interventions, 128–129
Interim assessments, 26, 27–28
Interruptions, 68
Intervention strategies, 61
Ireland, 96
IRIS Center, 135
Iyengar, S., 56, 58

Jamaica, 96–97
Johns Hopkins School of Education, ix, xi
Jones, L., 70
Jones, V., 70
Jöstl, G., 134

Katsipataki, M., 15
Kavanagh, K., 109
Kawanaka, T., 115
Kazdin, A. E., 93
Kingston, N., 15
Kirschner, P. A., 135
Kluger, A. N., 15
Knoll, S., 115

Know, understand, and be able to do (KUD)
    strategy, 2–4
Kokotsaki, D., 15, 120
Köller, O., 115
Koth, C. W., 103

Lake, C., 135
Lamb, S. M., 84
Language skills, 131–134
Large-scale assessments, 26–27, 30–31
Late starts, 68
Leaf, P. J., 103, 104
League tables, 46–47
Learning activities, 62
Learning environments, 67
Learning styles, 55–56
Lee, C., 15
Leffler, J. C., 56, 59
Leibniz Institute for Science and Mathematics
    Education (IPN), 111 (figure), 113
    (figure)
Lesaux, N., 135
Local assessments, 32–33
Lockwood, A. T., 58
Long-term commitments, 86
Lost time, 67–68
Low-stakes assessment, 48
Lüftenegger, M., 134
Lukas, J. F., 44

Machin, S., 49
Major, L. E., 15
Marshall, B., 15
Martin, A., 59
Martin-Forbes, P., 98
Maryland, 102
Mathematics achievement measures, 116–119
McDaniel, M., 55, 59
McNally, S., 49
McTighe, J., 34
Mehta, P. D., 134
Mentors, 88
Merrell, C., 119, 120
Meta-analytical reviews, 78, 83
Metacognitive activity, 36–37
Middle school students, 63–64
Miller, D. J., 119, 120
Mislevy, R. J., 44
Mitchell, M. M., 103
Monitoring systems, 127–128, 133
Moon, T. R., 5
Moyer, L., 93
Multiple-choice tests, 31

Multiple measures strategies, 16–19, 31
Multitiered prevention models, 61, 85, 126–129
    see also Positive Behavioral Interventions and
        Supports (PBIS) model

Nash, B., 15
National Assessment of Achievement in
    Mathematics, 114
National Assessment of Educational Progress
    (NAEP), 40
National Center on Response to Intervention, 127
National Council on Measurement in Education, 27
National Research Council, 89
National Technical Assistance Center, 102
Navo, M., 125
Neal, D., 48, 49
Nelson, S. R., 56, 59
New Zealand, 97
No Child Left Behind Act (2001), 30, 39
Nonnative English speakers, 131–134
Norway, 96

O'Connor, A., 59
Ohlsson, S., 44
Oliver, R. M., 79
Ongoing assessment, 3
On-time starts, 68
Oosterhof, A., 44
Organisation for Economic Co-operation and
    Development (OECD), 48
Ortiz, A., 134
Ostermeier, C., 115

Parenting programs, 94–97
Parrish, T., 125
Pas, E. T., 103
Pashler, H., 55, 59
Peabody College, 135
Peer assessment, 37
Peer-assisted learning strategies, 133
Peer collaborations, 71–72, 74
Peer tutoring, 117–119
Performance Indicators in Primary Schools
    (PIPS) project, 118
Performance measures
    cost-benefit analysis, 51–53, 52 (table)
    high-stakes assessments, 40–43, 47–48
    multiple measures approach, 18
Performance tasks, 18, 32
Persistence-plus, 87
Personalized interventions, 87–88
Person-centered classrooms, 80–83, 82 (table),
    87–88

Phonological processing, 131–132
Pietsch, M., 115
Pohl, A., 89
Poole, I., 75
Popham, W. J., 29
Porter, A. C., 112 (figure), 115
Portugal, 96
Positive Behavioral Interventions and Supports
    (PBIS) model, 99–103, 100 (figure)
Positive Behavior for Learning (PB4L)
    Action Plan, 97
Positive behavior support (PBS), 61, 106–107
Positive reinforcement practices, 90–93
Praise, 78, 91–92
Pre-assessment strategies, 2
Prenzel, M., 115
Preschool children, 105–108
Preventive discipline, 81
Primary prevention programs, 61
Proactive planning, 73
Problem solving, 41, 87
Procedural knowledge, 41
Professional collaborations, 71–72, 74
Professional development, 110–114, 111 (figure),
    112 (figure), 113 (figure)
Programme for International Student Assessment
    (PISA), 48, 110
Progress in International Reading Literacy Study
    (PIRLS), 110
Progress-monitoring systems, 127–128
Prosocial skills, 106
Purposefulness, 63

Quality instruction, 73

Randomized controlled trials (RCTs)
    Check & Connect program, 87
    parenting programs, 94–97
    peer tutoring, 119
    tiered intervention programs, 102, 103
Rapid pace of instruction, 69
Reading skills
    achievement measures, 116–119
    English language learners (ELLs), 131–134
Reebok, 55
Reid, J., 109
Relationships, 86, 88
Relevant research, 72, 78, 83, 87
Reschly, D., 79
Research-based/research-proven educational
    practices, 56–58, 73
Response to Instruction and Intervention (RTI²),
    126–129

Response to Intervention (RTI), 61, 85, 126
Rohani, F., 43, 44
Rohrer, D., 55, 59
Routines, 68
Rubrics, 8, 21–22, 32–33
Ruiz-Promo, M. A., 44

Sabornie, E., 61, 65
Sanfilippo, C., 44
Schober, B., 134
Schoolwide behavior intervention programs
    see Positive Behavioral Interventions and
        Supports (PBIS) model
Schoolwide support systems, 61
Schultz, S. E., 44
Science and mathematics professional development
    initiative, 110–114, 111 (figure), 113 (figure)
Scotland, 117–119
Screening tools, 126–127
Secondary school level, 63–64
Selective/secondary interventions, 61, 99–103,
    100 (figure)
Self-assessment, 17, 20–23, 36–37
Serrano, A., 115
Severson, H. H., 109
Shavelson, R. J., 44
Silva, O., 49
SINUS professional development program
    (Increasing Efficiency in Mathematics and
    Science Education)
    background information, 110–111
    content areas, 111 (figure)
    goals and objectives, 111, 112 (figure)
    preliminary results, 112–114
    program evaluation, 112, 113 (figure)
Skinner, B. F., 90
Slavin, R. E., xi, 69, 70, 135
Small-group support systems, 61
Social and emotional learning (SEL), 61
Social reinforcement practices, 91–92
Solano-Flores, G., 44
Spiel, C., 134
Standardized tests, 26, 30–31
Stiggins, R. J., 5
Stigler, J. W., 115
Stiller, B., 109
Stillwell, P., 44
Stout, K., 89
Student behavior
    Consistency Management & Cooperative
        Discipline (CMCD) model, 80–83, 82
        (table)
    effective classroom management practices, 62,
        76–78

First Step to Success (FS) program, 105–108
Incredible Years (IY) Teacher Classroom
    Management (TCM) program, 94–97
Positive Behavioral Interventions and Supports
    (PBIS) model, 99–103, 100 (figure)
positive reinforcement practices, 90–93
Student engagement, 73, 85–86
Student learning and achievement
    assessment strategies, 1–4
    co-teaching programs, 121–125
    England–Wales educational performance
        comparisons, 45–48, 46 (figure)
    feedback, 11–12, 13–14 (table), 14, 36–37
    formative assessment, 36–37
    multiple measures strategies, 17, 31
    reading and mathematics achievement
        measures, 116–119
    self-assessment strategies, 20–23, 36–37
Student Standards Folder, 33
Students with diabilities, 121–125, 132, 134
Student–teacher relationships, 94–97
Sugai, G., 99, 104, 109
Summative assessment
    characteristics, 7 (figure)
    differentiated classrooms, 3–4
    multiple measures strategies, 18, 19
Supplemental interventions, 128–129
Supporting Teachers And childRen in Schools
    (STARS), 95
Sustainable programs, 53
Sweller, J., 135

Tate, M. L., viii
Teacher Classroom Management (TCM)
    program, 94–97
Teachers
    formative assessment, 35–36
    professional development, 110–114,
        111 (figure), 112 (figure), 113 (figure)
    teacher-centered classrooms, 80–83,
        82 (table)
    teacher–student relationships, 94–97
Templeton, S. M., 84
Tertiary prevention programs, 61
Test preparation impacts, 30–31, 33
Thornton, L. A., 103
Thurston, A., 119, 120
Tiered intervention programs, 61, 85, 99–103,
    100 (figure), 126–129
Timperley, H., 10, 14 (table), 15, 38
Tolar, T., 135
Tomlinson, C. A., 5
Topping, K. J., 119, 120
Training opportunities, 73–74, 79, 110–114

Trends in International Mathematics and Science Study (TIMSS), 110, 114
Troutman, A. C., 93
Tutoring programs, 117–119
Tymms, P., 120

United Kingdom
  England–Wales educational performance comparisons, 45–48, 46 (figure)
  Fife Peer Tutoring Project, 116, 117–119
  parenting programs, 95
Universal prevention programs, 61, 85, 99–103, 100 (figure), 107
Universal screening assessments, 126–127
University of York, ix, xi
U.S. Department of Education, 39, 43, 87
U.S. National Center on Response to Intervention, 127
Uzuner, Y., 125

Validation, 43
Valtcheva, A., 23, 24
Vanderbilt University, 135
Vaughn, S., 130, 135
Vladeck, David, 55

Waasdorp, T. E., 103, 104
Wagner, H., 115

Wales
  England–Wales educational performance comparisons, 45–48, 46 (figure)
  parenting programs, 95
Walker, H. M., 109
Walsh, J. M., 125
Wang, X., 24
Wanzek, J., 130
Warburton, S., 59
Webster-Stratton, C., 94, 98, 109
Wehby, J. H., 79
Weinstein, C., 60, 65, 72, 75
Wendt, H., 115
Wexler, J., 130
What Works Clearinghouse, 57, 87
Wheater, R., 49
Wiggins, A., 119
Wiggins, G., 34
Wiley, E. W., 44
Wiliam, D., 5, 15, 26, 29, 38
Williams, M. E., 98
Williamson, G. L., 19
Wilson, D., 48, 49
Worth, J., 48, 49

Yoon, K. S., 112 (figure), 115

Ziegler, J. C., 135

CORWIN

A SAGE Company

The Corwin logo—a raven striding across an open book—represents the union of courage and learning. Corwin is committed to improving education for all learners by publishing books and other professional development resources for those serving the field of PreK–12 education. By providing practical, hands-on materials, Corwin continues to carry out the promise of its motto: **"Helping Educators Do Their Work Better."**